"Hey, Jack!"[1]
by Jan Kerouac

Hey, Jack! Hey, Jack! Is that you?
This is Jan Michele, your daughter.
Remember?
This is your daughter, remember?
I believe we met twice down in the Stew Pot.
Yeah, it's me.
I'd like to talk to the cat that begat me, you dig?
I heard your voice come over the line
From out there in black telephone universe land
And I felt like the RCA Victor dog.
Yeah.

Oh, to be a gleeful Mad Boy back to the mists of innocence
A Beat still incubating in the unsullied womb of Beathood
Where the only specters of doom were "two bald-headed cats
Who, like, could push a button and blow us all outta here, man!"
And now, those imagined antics of Khrushchev and Ike
Have long since dissolve in the serum of history.
Immortalized by Mad Magazine
Which I used to steal from the corner candy store
H bombs drawn in so many cartoons
It's become a cartoon, or at most the smallest measurement
Of nuclear firepower on earth.
No one seems to realize it, but I'll tell you a secret:

[1]This poem was written and partly improvised by Jan Kerouac for Marjorie Van Halteren's radio show "Captured Voices" on WNYC radio in New York City, in 1989. Jan
read it aloud against a backdrop of her father reading "Origins of the Beat Generation"
on a tape made at Hunter College in 1958.

The H bomb, I think, is the success secret of Japan.
Yeah.

If one of those sweet Beatitudinous Babes of yore
Had stood up and prophesied that in three decades
An Iranian fanatic would hold the entire publishing world hostage
If he had said
That there'd be Haitian drug gangs called posses in Kansas City
Or condoms advertised on TV
Computer viruses
Hypos handed out on street corners
If he had dared to suggest
That in the late 80s
Soviets would be more peace-minded than the Americans
And that there would be a huge hole in the ozone from spray cans
They would have put him in a straitjacket
And carted him away to an asylum.
And there, in the nuthouse,
He might have written a monstrous work of fantasy science fiction
To make George Orwell's *1984* look like the *Wizard of Oz* by
  comparison.

Ah, my poor father
He was such a Big Baby Noodlebrain
Too noodlebrained to exist in this world of geometric fear
Too animal saintly-headed
Too animal saintly-hooded
He was too saintly to crawl through those concrete rat mazes of
  tortured thought.
I know.
I'm the same kind of Baby Noodlebrain.
'Cause I can feel him in my bones

I'm getting to know him.
I'm getting to know Little Boy Blue from the inside out.

Racing down, down madness-awkward
On Madison Avenue to Madhattan today
Freezing in the cruel cold, I wrap myself up like an Arab
Blue hat and scarf like veils and, while rushing,
Caught a glimpse in store windows.
I looked like a mad Tuareg or Berber tribesman of the Sahara
Hurtling at full tilt on a horse
Or maybe even a camel
Turquoise shrouds and veils flapping in the hot desert wind.
Only this was cold city wind
Here on the other side of the Atlantic
Which reminded me of the ancient, sunken home
Of continental driftwood
Continental breakfasthood.

Ah, we humans must be a pretty hardy lot
to swarm all over this poor old globe, time after time
Strong as dynasties of cockroaches
In those tenements I used to live in.
Remember, Jack?
You came to visit me in a tenement.
I bet you didn't see any cockroaches
No, you were too drunk.
Well, never mind.
Anyway, so
You say,
All your fathers wore straw hats like W. C. Fields
Well,
I wish I could say that

But, you see,
My father was the Invisible Man
But I won't hold that against you.

Poem for Jack[1]
by Jan Kerouac

"Oh boy, that Jack
he really was a holy terror when he drank!"
says the neighbor, leaning on his rake,
standing amid fire-ant hills
in the Florida suburbs . . .
in alligator golfland.
Too many cars now—
where did he go?
That funny, disruptive chap,
my very own court jester who I never knew . . .
snatched from me by shadows—
sequestered by greedy fingers
too soon . . . so long ago.
"Yeah, that Jack—
he was a wild one all right!"
says the fat neighbor,
scratching his head in the cruel Florida sun . . .
"Ya know, he used to sit at that window
all night, by the standing lamp . . ."
I gaze at that window—trying
to see my father's silhouette
illuminated by a warm buttery glow . . .

[1]This poem was found among Jan's papers at her death.

hoping to recapture the magic . . .
but all I can see now, after 25 years
is dried weeds and concrete in the southern dayglare.
But then, when at long last
I sat in my father's swivel chair
before his desk . . .
the dark reddish wood spoke to me.
It said, "You belong here . . .
and we belong to you."
It was an amazing feeling
like a little boy sitting
in the cockpit of his father's plane—
finally I was at the controls.
My *daddy* . . . a word wholly unfamiliar
to my lips.
"Oh yeah! Jack came roarin' through that door—
he sure knew what he wanted!"
I stare at the framed brownish photo—
my eyes . . . my ears . . . the spitting image—
and the gatekeeper stands behind the screen door,
saying guiltily:
"Well, that's the way the cookie crumbles!"

Trainsong

Jan Kerouac

THUNDER'S MOUTH PRESS   NEW YORK

Published by
Thunder's Mouth Press
841 Broadway, Fourth Floor
New York, NY 10003

Originally published 1988 by Henry Holt and Company, Inc.

Library of Congress Card Catalog Number 98–85762

ISBN 1-56025-165-4

Designed by Jeffrey L. Ward

Manufactured in the United States of America.

For John Lamb Lash

Acknowledgments

Trainsong was originally published by Henry Holt and Company in 1988. Grateful acknowledgment is made to Brenda Knight of Conari Press, Bill Hurst of Publishers Group West, and Neil Ortenberg and Matthew Trokenheim of Thunder's Mouth Press for making this reissue possible. Special thanks to Marjorie Van Halteren who preserved Jan's partly-improvised poem "Hey, Jack!" on tape, and to Carol Tingle, the world's greatest transcriptionist, who returned it to the printed page with extraordinary fidelity.

—Gerald Nicosia

Publisher's Note

As of this printing there are still strong opinions on both sides of the debate concerning the Jack Kerouac estate. Jan Kerouac died believing her grandmother's will was forged and the Sampas family was handling the estate with greed and disrespect. Some people who were close to Jack Kerouac feel otherwise. Jan Kerouac's position was that many of her father's friends were unduly influenced by the financial power and publishing connections of the Sampas family. Others maintain that the Sampas's are decent and honest and are working in the best interests of Jack Kerouac and his legacy.

The significance of Jan Kerouac's career had to do with the facts that she was both a gifted writer and the daughter of a legend. The pathos flowing from her initial encounter with her drunken father on the lower east side is hard to escape throughout her two bruising autobiographical novels. We have added poems, photographs, journal entries, interviews, and articles on the estate battle to these new editions to give greater depth and information to the memoir-like quality of *Baby Driver* and *Trainsong*. It isn't easy for a child to escape from the shadow of a larger than life parent. It's harder still to shake off the abuse of an alcoholic father. Had Jack Kerouac chosen life over alcoholism maybe Jan could have had a reunion with the father she never knew. Instead she was left with memories of two brief encounters, her father's mystique, and the body of his work to speak to her. In a mental hospital at the age of fourteen Jan read *On The Road* for the first time. "I read it all in one night instead of ringing for another Seconal," she wrote in *Baby Driver*. She also wrote, "Now that I had a picture of what he'd been doing all this time, all over the country, it made more sense that he hadn't had the time to be fatherly."

In adding material to this addition concerning the ongoing court battle over the Jack Kerouac estate we have attempted to include information that deals with both sides of the issue. Regardless of the ultimate outcome, or the legitimacy of the claims or counterclaims from either side, we felt the general story of the lawsuit Jan initiated at the end of her life gives a certain perspective to the haunted, father-searching words that appear throughout both of her published works.

Neil Ortenberg, Publisher
New York
May 20, 1998

Is love worse living?

—James Joyce

Trainsong

1

Caught in a swirling undertow in the gulf of time . . . somewhere between the blackness of Allen's Victorian staircase in Boulder in October of '82 and a hot New York City tar rooftop strung with clotheslines in the early sixties . . . promise of lime Kool-Aid on the tongue . . . somewhere between misty volcanic hills of sugarcane in Costa Rica and the solid fleshlike adobes of New Mexico. Back and forth through thirty-three years of places, names, dates—but especially sounds, smells, and feelings. Shimmering visions, all the more real for their vintage. Is this what it's like to be dead? Like a ghost flitting about disguised as a hummingbird, savoring the old haunts of a colorful life, to have it all at one's fingertips?

We will meet again where our dream-tides crisscross. Perhaps Ti Jean—Daddy Jack—is floating this very moment through a Merrimack memory, and that is why he suddenly appears, youthful and

1

petulant on the bright sundunes of a Cape Cod seascape. Much later it will all become clear, like a stained-glass window seen from within a cathedral as someone sprays layers of dust off the outside with a garden hose. Much later could be right now, for all we know.

2

Rocky Mountain foothills loom purple behind Peter through the bathroom window as he wrings out Allen's socks. Near my elbow a lamp glows on the kitchen table, crowded all around by jars of spices and condiments, vitamins and hoisin sauce. Originally there were only a few bottles for ornament, but soon those attracted more of their kin to keep them company, sitting in moats of crumbs, cloaked with grease and dust.

The tabletop is gray Formica ringed with chrome, like the dinette sets of Puerto Rican families I knew in New York. Sometimes I think I'm still back there—amnesia playing hide-and-seek. But this is Boulder, Colorado, 1982. A rift in time between now and 1964 when I first met Allen and Peter on the Lower East Side of Manhattan. I was twelve then, scampering barefoot on the familiar filth of cobblestones. I'd run into Peter at the butcher's while shopping for my mother, or I'd see Allen with his great bushy beard at the fruit stand on Avenue C. We were across-the-street neighbors, and they were of my parents' generation, but age was no barrier in our melting pot.

"Hey, Allen, whadja do with the chicken?"

"Hah?" comes the inevitable reply from upstairs.

"The chicken—wheredja put it?"

Silence. Allen peeks around the corner, having descended the stairs to answer softly, "Ahh, I must have left it on the piano." He smiles, bemused and grandfatherly through a now-graying beard, eyes twinkling.

"Hah . . . on the piano. The piano." Peter grunts and mumbles absentmindedly into the living room. He returns with the plastic-clad carcass and slams it on the table, making the little jars of vitamins and honey rattle perilously. "So! We're having curry tonight. How 'bout that?" No longer yelling, Peter's voice returns to a soft growl, like the voices of junkies I've known who for some reason have lost their larynx power.

Allen winks at me and does a little jiggish dance.

"Oh boy, curried chicken!" He shuffles toward the cutting board and asks, "Can I help?"

"Uh, yeah, cut up some garlic," says Peter, lunging around housewifishly in white Bermudas, a thick gray ponytail hanging down his back.

I sit at the table, elbows resting on the cool Formica, content for the moment just to observe this oddly domestic scene . . . remembering Peter when his ponytail was honey blond and he wore red lace bikini panties around their apartment on East Tenth Street.

Now Peter is hovering over the table, slathering curry paste on chunks of raw fowl piled in a gold-rimmed glass punchbowl. Half of the jars surrounding the lamp have already toppled and the light bulb flickers off and on, its weak wiring jangled by his vigorous movements. Yellow splats appear everywhere, some even dripping down the table's chrome legs.

"Jesus! Aren't you cold?" Allen says, pulling on a sweater and closing the door.

"Nah," growls Peter, extracting a chicken liver and tromping barefoot out the door with the morsel dangling from his curried fingers.

"Well," Allen sighs, "I'll be up in my room writing. Call me when dinner's ready, okay?" He grabs teapot, cup, and strainer and goes upstairs.

I'm startled by an alarming staccato MEOW which seems to penetrate the house like a siren—it's Peter calling the cats. But by now they've all fled in terror. When he returns, he goes to the cupboard and takes out a huge bottle of sake—a size seldom seen outside the Boulder Buddhist community—furtively swigs, then slips it back into hiding.

I wonder: Did my father drink this way, stashing his bottle as if to conceal it from himself? Or did he guzzle openly for everyone to see?

From up yonder comes the tapping of Allen's typewriter. All is well in the Bluff Street household. It's beginning to feel like home.

Whizzing up pumpkin in the blender with evaporated milk and oil of cloves, I am spiraled back once more to that slum tenement on East Tenth . . . young Peter frying liver in great clouds of grease by an airshaft window, garbage cans six stories below. And his poor brother Julius, just out of a mental institution, still saturated with Thorazine, standing quietly in the corner picking at one crumb on his pants' leg for hours on end, never saying a word. Benevolent Allen sitting before some other, long-lost typewriter, a quart of beer at his side instead of tea . . .

Back on Bluff Street, after a dinner of coriander- and turmeric-ridden chicken, cardamom-specked coleslaw, and clove-redolent pie, we three are positively mentholated with spices. Allen repairs to the piano to practice for an upcoming reading at the Mercury Café in Denver, and I'm still in the kitchen with Peter.

"So, ahh, Janny. What didjoo and your father talk about that first time you met, for the blood tests in Brooklyn?"

"Oh. Hmmm, let me see. . . ." I am unprepared for this sudden casual interrogation. "Well, actually, not much at first. I mean he was talking to the lawyer and my mother mostly."

Peter shifts from one foot to the other while washing the dishes, somehow managing to spew whole bubbles from the sink. I'm mesmerized.

"So what'd he *say?*"

"Well, we were sitting in the bar, and I was watching a TV up in the corner by the ceiling. An astronaut went up in space that day."

"So what did your father say? C'mon now!" Peter demands, ignoring the dishes now, but not looking at me, just nodding his head slightly, eyes closed, as if listening to some inner jazz riff. He seems impatient.

"Well, you see, I'm trying to remember. It was so long ago and not much was said. Oh, I know. He told my mother, 'You always used to burn the bacon.' It was nice to hear them talk like that. It was the first time I'd ever heard my parents speak to each other. . . ."

"Mmmm, yeah. *Yeah.*" Peter nods in affirmation, his eyes still shut and waiting for more.

"You know—I really don't remember anything he said to me in the bar at all . . . or even later in the doctor's office."

"You *gotta* remember!" He yells, pacing the kitchen floor, his full voice range coming through now. "You only talked to him twice!"

"Once on the phone, too."

"So, only three times. You gotta remember what happened— it's very important. It's all in there somewhere!"

I am taken aback by Peter's sudden obsession with what my father said to me—and a little defensive, especially since my memory of him is mostly visual.

6

"Okay, I concede. The one thing I definitely recall him saying, when we got back to my neighborhood, was, 'Where's the nearest liquor store?' I *know* he said that."

"Okay. So then what?" Peter opens his eyes and leans against the refrigerator, arms folded like Mr. Clean.

"So I took him to the one on Tenth Street by the park."

"There's no liquor store on Tenth Street. Never was one!"

"*Peter.* You know. The one around the corner from Sid's candy store."

"Nah, nah, 'sno liquor store there."

"But there *is*. I remember because I took him by the hand and led him right to it!"

"You must mean the one up on Twelfth."

"No, I'm telling you, this one is between Sid's and the library—across from the park where the crosstown bus stops—it's got those dark-green diamond gratings in front—"

"Nah, nah."

Now I'm getting mad. "*Peter!* I know it's there. I remember clearly that my father bought a bottle of Harvey's Bristol Cream sherry there. I'll never forget that!"

"Atta girl."

"On the way over there I saw some neighborhood kids who asked, 'Dat your father?' and I nodded proudly. He was so shy. . . ."

"Nope, couldn't be there—no, no no," Peter persists.

"Oh, it's there all right, printed right smack on my memory screen—the picture of him standing there in his baggy pants and 'survival hat,' holding that brown-paper sack, the green trees of Tompkins Square Park looming behind him, a few wisps of dark-brown hair, same color as mine, hanging down on his forehead, his lower lip protruding, and such blue, blue eyes. . . ."

I can't go on. My own blue eyes are filling with tears. Pretending to be mad, I storm into the bathroom for some tissue.

"Yeah, I know the one you mean. You're right, there *is* a liquor store on Tenth Street." Without another word, Peter begins scrubbing the curry splats off the table as energetically as he put them there.

I trudge up the Victorian staircase to my room, feeling pleasantly exhausted—slightly dizzy and disoriented, like I've just been under a waterfall in an inner tube. I collapse motionless on the bed, but my mind keeps moving, swirling in whirlpools of images, my father incessantly reemerging from an ocean of visions and fantasies . . . I see him peeling black plastic from the neck of the sherry bottle; melancholy clowning for my twin half sisters. And six years later, the second and last meeting, seated in a rocking chair in his native Lowell, guzzling a bottle of whiskey . . .

Then it dawns on me. That sly devil Peter was deliberately goading me. All that craziness about the liquor store not being there was just to make me think harder and dredge up lost memories. And it *worked*.

I drift into cradled blackness with the happy realization that these strange fellows are far wiser than I know. There is sweet comfort in being guided by oddball angels . . .

3

The Kittitas valley stretched across central Washington State like a vast green chenille bedspread. It had soaked up great quantities of rain that April of 1974. Soon May would begin. Magpies swooped past the ditches, making black-and-white flashes of wings against sky.

The weeping willows where John and I had hung Yucatan hammocks in 1971 were still there. I was amazed to see them, but then I remembered: Trees don't go away like people do. Unless they're cut down, they just grow bigger.

The house we had lived in when we were married was still there too. The sight of its familiar fake brown brick siding stirred up visions of those days . . . John building a greenhouse for tomato seedlings . . . me feeding the cat . . . I wondered if the house had felt deserted when we left. Now there were other people living in it.

People with a dog. The house didn't seem to mind, but then it had no choice.

I hadn't seen my mother or brother for three years, except for a brief chaotic visit when I had breezed up from Phoenix, fresh from the massage parlors. At the time my main objective had been to shock everyone—and it had worked. Even my own mother had hardly recognized me through the façade of dyed, teased hair, hot-pants, and spike heels: the whorish cocoon I'd spun around myself.

But now in the spring of '74 I'd long since given up on that shock appeal. As I saw it, four months in South America had changed me considerably. Filled with new experiences and saturated with jungle essence of the Peruvian Amazon, I had a scorching desire to speak Spanish with my mother. But I soon discovered that the halting Cuban she'd picked up from busboys in the fifties was not the brand of Spanish I craved.

In my brother David's room I gazed out the west-facing window, across pale green fields. From here in Kittitas you could see Mount Rainier. But, I remembered, as you drove toward Ellensburg it always sank like a huge snow-sun into the horizon. This phenomenon of perspective always baffled me. It was like goals: they too seemed to evaporate the closer you got to them. *April is the foolest month*, I whispered to myself.

In the midst of the familial chatter and cluttered eccentricity of my mother's house, it was hard to believe that only a week before I had been in Lima, Peru. Waking up by the wood stove, my sleepy eyes would scan the dusty Britannicas, red curtains, wooden chair with a gash in the seat which my mother used for a sawhorse, the blackened turquoise-enamel coffee pot—and often I could not remember where I was. For four months I had been surrounded by high-strung South Americans—even came very close to merging totally with them. And now, back home with my tiny family of impoverished New Yorkers, I was feeling a measure of culture shock, secure yet misplaced.

In the morning David left for school with a pocketful of Peruvian *soles de oro*, Guatemalan *quetzals*, and Nicaraguan *cordobas* for show and tell. My mother and I made coffee in the old blue pot on the wood stove and talked.

"It got down to forty below zero here in January, you know. We had to sleep in four layers of clothes and keep both stoves roaring all night and most of the day."

"Wow—that's damn cold! You poor things. And to think where *I* was in January . . . the *Amazon*."

My mother sighed as she poured the coffee.

"Yes, Jan, I think a lot about where you are—and it's almost always too far away."

"So how did you survive in here with so little insulation?"

"Just barely. Every morning for a week I knocked ice off the *inside* of the door before David could get out to school."

"With that crowbar, I bet." I nodded toward the familiar tool in the corner as a vision flashed in my mind—my mother at twenty-four knocking chunks of plaster off a tenement brick wall.

"Yup, but that's not the same one I had in New York," she said, reading my thoughts.

"God, do you realize that probably at the same moment you and David were stoking the stoves with chair legs and pulling on another pair of socks over the first three—"

"You were lying in a sweltering humid A-frame hut next to an Argentinian madman!" She finished my sentence while I guzzled a gulp of coffee.

After hours of indulgent caffeinated chatting, I went out and climbed over the twisted fence between my mother's backyard and the backyard of the house where John and I had lived when we were married. The sight of the willows and the fake brick siding rekindled all sorts of memories . . . our ménage à trois with Hilary, musical hammocks on warm nights, the languid Indian feasts of September. How strange to be an alien on once familiar ground—the dog that lived here now began to bark at me. I climbed back over the fence and pondered what might have happened if I had stayed there with John. . . . It had been my decision to leave, his decision to stay. And after all, there had been more cavorting and wild things to do. . . .

Weeding the strawberry patch later, my mother and I talked some more—this time about David, and his marvelous vocabulary, so large for a nine-year-old. She told me about his recent experiments with water bottles, tape recorders, and magnifying glasses. Hard to believe our budding boy genius had been such a sickly runt of a baby, several times had almost died from asthma attacks. And now our hearts swelled with relief to see him growing up, healthy and handsome and tall. We reminisced about the times when I, a precocious fifteen, carried my infant brother through Tompkins Square Park in New York and people thought he was *my* baby.

4

Blissfully absorbed in the task of planting peas, in a sort of trance that Monday afternoon, the sight of David shuffling down the alleyway with his schoolbooks—all scuffed up and crying, with a black eye—caused something to snap inside of me.

It was the first time I could remember feeling such a pure form of anger coursing through my veins, a protective rage over blood kin. This was the stuff wars were made of. All I could see as I stormed toward the trailer court was the face of my sweet gentle brother being pounded over and over by the cruel fist of a worthless redneck bully.

I hadn't a drop of reason left in my head, no hesitation in the steps that brought me up to the door.

BASH, BASH, BASH—my fist on white aluminum. The door opened and a pasty-faced boy of about ten emerged from the foodish interior.

"You Stubby?" I demanded, unwavering in my fury.

"Yeah, dat's me," he shrugged, mouth full of some puffy orange snack—*probably Cheetos.*

"You beat up my little brother David," I accused blatantly, surprised at my own voice that sounded so crude and street-tough. Simultaneously I grabbed him, shaking him by the neck and collar with wild adrenaline relish—*kind of like it feels to smash loaves of Wonder bread.*

"Yeah, so what?" He sputtered, uncertain in stockinged feet on the rickety porch.

"You better not *touch* him again!" I bullied with emphasis.

Just then, who should appear but *Mama Bear*—a scrapping trucker woman in her mid-forties with dyed red hair who spent most of her time carousing in Kelly's Tavern. *Lynette.* I had forgotten about her.

"You live in that trailer house over there?" Lynette drawled, conveniently mistaking me for the teenaged Chicano girl next door.

I computed this bit of accidental flattery, then switched gears to a certain brand of poor people's pride. "Hell, I don't live in no *damn* trailer house! I live in a *real* shack!"

"Well—lady or girl, or whatever you are"— *BLAM.*

Next thing I knew, Mama Bear swung a heavy-handed paw down on my presumptuous head and sent me reeling and toppling off the three steps. *Still on my feet, though.*

"Git off ma property an' *stay* off!"

I turned back, defiant as ever and determined not to let on that I'd even noticed her brain-scrambling blow.

"Well, your son just better keep his hands off my brother or you'll be hearin' from *me!*" I blustered, dizzy but walking tall, backing slowly away, my head tingling and roaring on the left side. I sauntered shackward, knowing full well that I'd been in the wrong but not caring. Glad I had followed my instincts for once. And suffered a battle scar for David.

5

I awoke to find myself alone in the shack . . . voices outside. It was beastly hot. My head still hurt. I listened vacantly to my mother's bell-like explanations of her gardening methods. Who was she talking to? With mild curiosity, I slipped into shorts and a scanty halter top and emerged without even brushing my hair.

A boyish brown-skinned man was standing in the strawberry patch, shyly watching my mother dig out plants for him. He followed her movements closely, turning his head like a cat, saying nothing, seemingly hypnotized. She went on and on about the strawberries, telling him where she would put them if she were he, but he wasn't paying attention.

When I came out into the morning sun, all disheveled like a coquettish floozy, the man's eyes shifted to me.

"Oh, Alphonso, this is my daughter, Jan."

He flashed me some white teeth and glimmering brown eyes and then looked down at the weeds near his feet.

"Hi, Alphonso . . ." I offered him a hand and he squeezed it nervously. *Smooth hands of a lazy mechanic.* I was not awake enough to be nervous, but felt just the right amount of magnetism simmering beneath the surface to become intrigued.

"Me encantan las fresas," I ventured boldly, using the strawberries as an excuse to chat in Spanish, and waited to see if he'd bite. His mouth formed a synaptic recognition, and out came a soft laugh.

"Si, que lindas las fresas," he responded, confirming our mutual interest in strawberries. Character lines gave away his age, a very boyish thirty-four—a nice mixture of jaded innocence. I was feeling quite wolfish in my fox's disguise.

"Su Mama es muy amable darme esas plantas," Alphonso went on, putting the icing on the cake by complimenting my mother. Having established our secret tongue so early in the game, we went back to English, already plotting in wordless glances to meet each other. Soon. Somewhere.

One sun-dappled afternoon in early May I took a stroll down by the tracks. Avoiding heaps of sugar beets dumped by a freight train, I cat-walked the rail. Warm breezes played in and about my thighs through a flimsy red silk dress. *He should be along soon.* A memory vision of his eyes flashing brown and full of mischief flickered before me. *"Alla, cerquita del ferrocarril,"* he'd said, we'd meet by the train. The Spanish language had by now begun to symbolize a certain type of experience: one corner of my universe that was set aside for flings with men—Latin men.

From behind me, through tall poplars lining an irrigation ditch, came a rumbling. I felt the vibrations travel into my feet via the rail. I peeked backward through my hair: a rearview mirror trick developed in New York for spying on would-be attackers or anyone following too persistently.

An old Chevy pickup was nearing, and sure enough Alphonso was at the wheel, barechested. Feigning surprise, I turned around as he pulled up alongside the tracks, engine pulsating in a deep chortle.

"Hey, *Preciosa, ven aca, da me un beso,*" he coaxed softly, as if to tame a wild mare, when he asked for a kiss.

Odd how a truck can seem to emit the same charm as the man driving it. I mused, pretending not to know him at first. I continued to keep my balance as he purred slowly along. This preliminary courting was fun—suspenseful. I wanted it to go on for as long as possible—all of two minutes in the end. Those warm breezes, made even warmer by the Chevy's engine, combined with Alphonso's sweet talking were too much, and I hopped down from the rail into his waiting door. We held hands as he drove to Fergusen's Pond, communication dwindling to feverish glances as I sat closer, sliding over the hot leather seat. . . .

Was this how teenagers are supposed to feel at drive-in movies? I had totally missed that part of growing up. And so, Fergusen's Pond became the drive-in movie which we ignored as twilight turned to chill spring night and the final first moves were made, tearing off clothes, squeezing into awkwardly tangled pretzels under the steering wheel, skin against skin in a festival of sensual perspiration—deaf to our own symphony of gasps and blind to the incongruity of four feet on the windshield. Another animalistic affaire was born.

6

I had forgotten how it was to live in such a small town . . . where a gravel Main Street begins with a faceless laundromat and ends four blocks later in a tangle of farm machinery and two taverns. Here in Kittitas (Yakima Indian for The Eating Place) people really did go so far as to guess what color panties you were wearing by what they saw hanging on your clothesline.

Most of that summer of 1974 I spent in a blur of cheap wine—Nawico white port, Alphonso's favorite. We drove the width and breadth of the valley in a sloshed stupor in various vehicles, went swimming in the Columbia River, slept under reeling stars and dark bushes. We went fishing in the hills—caught a whole sack of trout and then lost every single one stumbling over rocks on the way back to the car, but it made a good story at the tavern that night anyway.

Sometimes we'd go in his '54 Chevy pickup of rusty robin's-egg blue, and sometimes in my '61 Olds Cutlass, which I'd gotten for free—found it abandoned up on Mnashtash Ridge, had it towed, and named it Fred. But sometimes, when we got really desperate, he'd risk picking me up in the family car, a white station wagon. And it was then that I knew in my bones, even through the alcoholic haze, that I was living too dangerously.

I barely missed becoming an alcoholic that summer. Reeling along with Al I felt we were two monstrous adolescents, parking by stagnant ponds and necking in mosquito-ridden sunsets. We had the makings of a truly schizoid relationship. Through the gauzy film of booze Alphonso appeared beautiful to me—smooth-skinned, handsome and brown, with liquid dark eyes, a sensual lover with whom I could speak Spanish. But then the hangovers would smack us down and we'd awake in underbrush by the roadside or in some seedy hotel room, face to face with the ugliness of our debauchery. At times like these I could see Al for what he truly was, a drunk whose liver was almost gone . . . *just like my father before he died.*

In September Alphonso and I got jobs picking potatoes for twenty-five dollars a day. It was back-breaking labor, dragging the burlap sacks along the ground between our legs until they weighed over fifty pounds. Then his wife kicked him out of the house and, having no place to live, he began hanging around in the alleyway behind our shack at night. We could hear him quite clearly out there, as he stumbled around with his bottle of white port, calling "Juana, please! I *need* you—Juana!" through the poorly insulated wall. This reminded my mother of some seedy rendezvous she'd had in Juarez, Mexico, in 1957 when she divorced my father. When Dick Brown, the one cop in Kittitas, started routine prowls down the block in his squad car to keep an eye on Alphonso, who was passed out in the woodpile, and Alphonso's son began bullying David at school, I realized the small-town scandal had gone too far.

Coming to my senses one crisp autumnal day, I drove my sputtering flame into Ellensburg, to a house where two young men from New York lived. They'd said he could stay with them—but they weren't home. Several trips back and forth through the valley later, they were finally home, and I finally dumped him off.

When I returned to Kittitas Alphonsoless that evening, my mother heaved a deep sigh of relief and said, "Ahh yes, Jan . . . those were the days. The days of wine and potatoes."

7

October on the railroad tracks . . . an earthbound medley of fall colors showing up in smashed rot of leaves—orange-pop, brown-cow, red-nest maple all packed into black sediment of creosote. Fossils of the future. Train gravel reposes grayly under still skies as darkening solstices approach.

A fake brick siding house squats alone in the dry brown grass, describing its square within a square lot on the wrong side of the tracks. Wet shiny street reflects slate-blue twilight. Tactile pebbles crackle undersoul. October is running out in the winds of time machination. All the soiled spuds have been grabbed up by metal spikes and metacarpals, and now the empty fields yawn in wait for snow on the cloud-hung plateau.

Here in Dogtown at the end of squash-moons . . . locomotives clang past, punching deep rhythms into the jawbone of Earth's heart, our hearth. Clanging and pummeling in solid affirmation of what is yet to come—the song is sung. The stage is set, a brown-gold theater of near night. No actors, no potatoes, not even a dog to roam the street. No one's home. You can feel it between your teeth, it's so solid. Everything is either rotting, precipitating, or freezing with dense mineral presence. Crunch. Feel it? It's a rock bottom holiday. It's Halloween.

Darker and darker. The Cascades were deep violet dunce caps and Mount Rainier was sinking into a salmon glow in the west, dropping faster and faster as I drove closer. All Hallow's Eve tonight. But as I scanned the far-spoking fields full of cows and farmhouses which appeared to crawl backward like glowworms along the valley, the scenery was no more ghostly than usual.

Rattling along in Fred, my Cutlass, down the dim blue road, just a serpentine hump between cattail ditches, I rumbled over the diagonal tracks where the freight train cuts through, the very same rails I had tightrope-walked that first sultry afternoon with Alphonso six months before—and, I recalled with a shiver, also the same crossing where John had barely escaped death one night in a head-on collision three years earlier. Except for this one spot which always gave me a little adrenaline rush, like the fear of a boogeyman under the bed, driving the two-lane Kittitas Highway was as uneventful as sewing on an old Singer sewing machine, the only object to hug the seam. Soon, though, Ellensburg broke the monotony by spreading out its warmly lit quartz iodine streets, and I was bumping over a different set of tracks—already in Dogtown.

And there was the little house where the two bachelors from New York lived—so many times dark and deserted when I was trying to deliver Alphonso—this time bursting with light, that wonderful orange-yellow kind that electric bulbs emanate through the windows of a house at twilight, when outside is all a perfect contrast of violet blue.

Alphonso had stayed only three days with them, and then returned home to his wife and kids in Kittitas. How odd to think that if it hadn't been for Alphonso, I probably would never have met Bertrand and Melvin.

I lugged my old stereo out of the car (earlier I had climbed over mountains of boxes in my mother's shed to retrieve the dusty old thing, stockpiled for several years since John and I split up) and up the steps of the little house in Dogtown, feeling a bit like the Frankenstein monster by the cottage in the forest when he peered in the window and saw the old man playing a violin. But this was Melvin playing his saxophone.

It was also Melvin who opened the door and stood there for some moments in a frenzy of indecision.

"Oh—uhh, hi! Gee . . . wow, you brought it—*music!* Uh, well, I ahh . . ."

"Jeezus, Mel, get outta the way! Hi, c'mon in. Here, let me take that." Bertrand came to the rescue, shaking his head while Melvin began throwing things helter-skelter in a feeble attempt to help make room for the stereo.

"Heah, wanna caramel?" Bertrand said to me in casual Newyorkese, bringing back a wave of nostalgia. Something rare was happening to me at that moment: the fragrance of linseed oil from Bertrand's paints, the sound of "Harlem Nocturne" wailing from the tape deck, taste of caramel melting on my tongue, vision of ultramarine swirls on the canvas, and the feeling of the gas heater warming the small of my back—all five senses fulfilled *at once*. And as I watched these two characters bickering goodnaturedly, hooking up my old stereo, I felt safe. I knew I'd found some kindred souls after such a long summer of blind, senseless debauchery.

Under a bare dangling kitchen light bulb in the tiny house in Dogtown that Halloween night, I was happily pinned against the stove by a Japanese army officer screaming, "We too have six-footers, as you call them!" This was only one of many quasi-sadistic dramatizations that threw me into fits of giggling. Bertrand brought out his *num chuks* and whirled them through the air with a flamboyance that was mind-boggling—even though he did smash the lamp. If he was trying to impress me, he succeeded. For I was in the mood to be Silly Putty.

Meanwhile, Melvin was holding court from his throne: a burgundy velvet monstrosity complete with sprung springs and shiny black armrests where the velvet was worn away by grimy hands. An art deco pedestal ashtray wobbled precariously before him, heaped with Camel straight butts and threatening to fall over every time someone passed by on the creaky old floorboards.

"Hey, listen to *this*, man!" Melvin was saying to nobody in particular. "This is *truly* avant-garde!"

I WANNA BOOGLERIZE YA, BABY.

He sang along in a perfect raspy imitation of Captain Beefheart, in a voice almost identical to his own anyway. Sitting enshrouded in a perpetual fog of Camel smoke, he slid album after album out of his four-foot-long record collection. Now he was playing the disc jockey *par excellence*, his favorite role—something he'd been dying to do for weeks since his own stereo had gone on the blink. Melvin was a fish tossed back into water.

After spraying the kitchen ceiling with Olde English "800" ale and grinding candy corn into the linoleum, Bertrand and I needed a change of scene. We took a stroll outside, leaving Melvin to his stereophonic bliss. We walked and walked through crisp wind and crumpled leaves, a thin sliver of a crescent moon playing hide-and-seek through black twiggy branches, till we arrived at an old deserted house. Bertrand led me by the hand up a narrow staircase to a little room. I smiled at him in wondering disbelief in the bluish unearthly light from a street lamp. The moon was too new to cast any glow.

"Just as I thought—it's still here," he said, brushing leaves off a small mattress on the floor and closing the window.

"This was my room last year. We can sleep here tonight."

24

"Alone at last!" I playacted, as we collapsed on the mattress together. We lay there for some time, face to face, trading histories of New York, attempting to figure out whether our paths had ever overlapped or come close or crisscrossed in that great city, equally beloved by both of us.

As I watched Bertrand in the half dark it dawned on me how relieved I was to be the audience for a change, instead of the performer. Here was someone whose tales were even more amazing than mine, and a fellow New Yorker to boot. I allowed myself to be spellbound. Now he launched into his story about Melvin, and as he did so he *became* Melvin, making his voice nasal and raspy and rolling his eyes. I could even see thick-rimmed glasses, a hairier face. This guy had a real knack for contorting himself into just about any shape.

"So they'd taken Melvin down into the bowels of the hospital, Payne Whitney, that is, to get fitted for new glasses. His old ones had finally bit it the night he was admitted. And there he was, standing in the awful pink hallway like a wild animal. Even without glasses old Mel spotted a square of real sunlight way down the corridor, an open door to the OUTSIDE. Without a moment's hesitation he bolted. Ran like hell all the way through the park to the other side, never looking back till he hit the West Side."

"Wow, that's a long way."

"Yeah, Melvin always was a fast runner. And that time it really paid off—saved his ass. You know, he was the first person *ever* to escape from Payne Whitney Mental Hospital."

"Quite a distinction!"

"Yeah. So poor Melvin couldn't go home, or risk being sent back by his father. So for a while I just rode in from Queens on the F train and we hung out together like twin bums in the doorways of Manhattan. I couldn't let him do that all *alone*. He had nobody. And I couldn't take him home to my dad either."

"So how did you wind up here, in Ellensburg, Washington, of

all places?" I felt kind of silly asking him this, the question everyone else always asked *me*.

"Ahh . . . the saga continues. Let's see . . . next, this oddball Rogue Blackson from Colorado shows up in town. He was starting some kind of a school for boys, or that's what he told our fathers anyway. He managed to get them both to shell out a ton of money, and then he took us to Morocco. All we did was carry his bags everywhere—we were his slaves. And he fed us nothing but beets till our piss turned red."

"Why beets?"

"Because they were the cheapest. Ahh, but then we fell in with Mahmudi, Fatima, and Sadiya. They were *great*. Melvin and I were embraced by a whole family of Moroccans. Rescued temporarily from Blackson. I fell in love with the daughter, Sadiya . . . wanted to marry her. . . ." He trailed off dreamily and there was a moment of silence.

"Then, we had to come back. Our visas were running out, et cetera, et cetera. Rogue's next scheme, our next semester of finishing school, which nearly finished us, was Gold Hill, Colorado. There, Melvin and I lived in a tiny shack with no running water, next to a pigpen. Rogue had left us to fend for ourselves with two bull dykes, Mary and Rose. We had to work for them—they were like Marine sergeants! They wore plaid shirts and had *whiskers*. Made us chop wood all day. 'Heaaaargh! Slop them hogs, boy! I'm Rose—better not mess with me or I'll stomp yer bones!'

"It was twenty below zero and we had to go out and shit in eight feet of snow in the middle of the night—with pigs knocking us over!"

I had to catch my breath from laughing.

"Well, there was one consolation in that godforsaken dump—a big black pig named 'Nig.' He was my favorite. Boy, I sure loved that pig. Ole Nig." He shook his head in genuine fond reflection. "We graduated just barely from that class—and then there was the barbershop here in the Burg. You know the rest."

"But what exactly did Rogue want you to do in that place?"

"Live there—in the back, all winter with no heat, that's all . . . oh, and sell those stupid paperbacks. We were supposed to be converting it into a bookstore, but it had been a barbershop for so long that no one took it seriously. The row of barber chairs bolted to the floor didn't help, I suppose, and the only customer we ever got was your 'pal' Alphonso. He'd stumble in occasionally from the Highline Tavern next door and buy some cowboy novel that he couldn't read anyway. But finally Mel and I wised up and moved out of that dump—got this house in Dogtown."

"Isn't it amazing, that we quite possibly passed each other on streets and in subways in New York many times, but it took all this time and far-reaching zigzags and *Alphonso* for us to finally meet!"

We stayed in the empty house all night, talking and dozing and cuddling like kittens. And as dawn encroached its pale slate glare upon the dusty windowpanes, we also tried wrestling like leopards for a while—some intimate gymnastics to entertain the ghosts.

Along the railroad tracks under scarlet break of day we held hands, passing over footbridges and through cattails. He was Christopher Robin and I was Anne—the sketchy weeds in morning mist harked back to A. A. Milne books of my childhood, and I could almost hear the singsong voice of my mother calmly narrating between intermittent gulps of coffee. That morning was somehow magical—November first, All Saints' Day.

Nearly a year passed. I left my mother and brother in Kittitas and moved into the Dogtown house. The three of us lived in a comfortably warped version of *Leave It to Beaver*, a down-and-dirty version invented by Bertrand in an attempt to exorcise all things *wholesome*. He had a unique complex about anything that struck him as "wholesome," a word that his mother had evidently been overly fond of. This complex of his had severe ramifications; for instance, birds singing outside in the morning would fling him into

27

paroxysms of horror: "Goddamn fuckin' birds! Shut up! Oh! They're so WHOLESOME!" He would writhe and giggle morbidly and cover his head with the blankets. The only way I could imagine his problem was to remember how I feel if I accidentally flip on Mister Rogers on the TV—but magnified 100 times. One night I made hot chocolate and Bertrand nearly went off the deep end—said he couldn't stand to hear the sound of hot chocolate being poured into a mug. It was *too wholesome for words.*

So the next time he went into the bathroom to take a piss, I called in to him, "Hey Bertrand, what's that wholesome sound I hear in there? Are you pouring hot chocolate into a mug on a cold winter's night?"

"What? What are you talking about?" He was incredulous at first, but then he couldn't help but notice the similarity.

"Hey! That's amazing! It sounds the same!"

From then on whenever I made hot chocolate (which I called cocoa) for Ward and the Beave, all he had to do was remember that it sounded like someone pissing in a toilet and he was all right. I thought he was cured. But what to do about the birds?

Melvin had no such complex. He was in seventh heaven, playing baby bear. Bertrand and I would often embrace in the doorway and gaze fondly at Melvin in his burgundy velvet chair, playing with his toy records, and we'd sigh—"Our son." Then Melvin would look up through his thick glasses and snort in his raspy Beefheart voice, "Hi, Mom, hi, Dad!" Or sometimes when he was feeling particularly energetic, he'd actually rouse himself from the chair, pull down his pants, and shine us a moon. And, indulgent parents that we were, we'd simply shake our heads and go to bed, while he played on into the night with Billie Holiday and McCoy Tyner and Fats Domino.

8

We had always heard the roar and clank of the cannery on still summer nights, and held our noses while passing the heaped-up carrot waste in November. We had been dimly aware of strangely attired old women pouring out into the parking lot as we shuffled lazily across the tracks on our way home to Dogtown.

Now it was time for us to join the ranks of the terminally employed. The first night at Twin City Foods, Melvin, Bertrand, and I arrived at the old silo tracks in mandatory galoshes—slick, black, knee high, obtrusively new and uncontaminated by corn. Trudging reluctantly through the entranceway, we were glad to have jobs, but mourned for our lost freedom. The black gummy pavement in front of the cannery reminded all three of us of New York subway platforms.

After punching communion wafers at the time clock and sprinkling holy water at the factory sink, we were ready. Armed with earplugs, hairnets, visors, white plastic aprons with our names magic-markered in front for everyone to see, and yellow rubber gloves to match the corn, we rows of workers stood dutifully along the conveyor belt, facing each other. It was empty and motionless so far, but everything buzzed in a low hum, about to begin.

We were like giant kindergarteners waiting for the teacher to bring crayons for our paper. Just as I was thinking this, lo and behold, down came the first bits of corn. But this didn't resemble any corn I'd ever seen; it was black and stunted with blight. So my accidental prophecy came true—the pale damp suface of the conveyor belt became our paper, and the blighted corn our crayons. All sorts of obscenities came rolling past—corn smut, literally—scrawled by the younger employees. This gave the prudish old lifers the task of erasing it all with gloved hands while looking down the belt, aghast, to see who its authors might be. But—CRASH BOOM CLANK—before any unrest could germinate, an avalanche of steaming yellow native American hybrids came twisting and jostling right into our waiting rubber gloves.

Bertrand was opposite me on the line. He had become a stiff robot toy in his black stocking cap (he refused to wear a hairnet) and was wagging his head from side to side, making the topknot flop ridiculously. Several workers exploded in deafened mirth at his clowning—even the gestapolike matrons who came to reprimand him laughed. No one, it seemed, was immune to his collection of uncanny grimaces created with plastic mouth and doll-bright eyes. He had already established himself as the official joker of the cannery.

As I watched Bertrand reeling out his repertoire, doing the same acts over and over for fresh audiences, it began to dawn on me that our whole relationship was based on his clowning and my being entertained. As I grabbed and groveled in the ever-moving pile of slippery yellow cobs, corralling them point side first into the cutters, I wondered what this could mean. If I ever ceased to laugh at his jokes, would it be over? I saw him goofing for a cute blond in a red scarf . . . *What's the difference? She can giggle just as well as I can. . . .*

But this train of thought was disastrous to pursue—the night had only just begun. I shook the demons of jealousy out of my head, or at least scrambled them beyond recognition for the time being. There were unpleasant enough sensations to deal with already: stinging feet, waterlogged fingers, blurred vision, the stench of rotting corn stuck in the teeth of machinery mixed with the smell of freshly steamed cobs—it was enough to make a lot of people never want to eat corn again. Add to all this the simultaneous motions of cobs going by to the right and, below on a smaller belt, kernels teeming to the left, and it was potentially nauseating.

Fortunately I had always had a stomach of iron, and this motion reminded me of something else—something nautical, magical. At first it was hard to pinpoint, but then it came to me—the *Amazon.* The speed of the conveyor belt was like the slow drift of a canoe down a river. If I blurred my vision just right, the heaps of corn appeared to be a jungle river bank, and I could trick myself into thinking that I was the one moving . . . leaning over the railing of an old riverboat—

LUNCHTIME!

I nearly fell overboard—someone was screaming in my plugged ear. Just one of the old "lifer" ladies, coming to relieve my post. On corn-sea legs I staggered down the slippery metal stairs to the big basin full of soapy water where we all stopped to scrub the corn flecks off our arms.

I was just in time to witness a very odd sight: Melvin, totally encrusted with little flecks of corn, from his rhinecorn-studded hairnet to his arms to his galoshes, even his *glasses. How could he see?* Everyone stopped scrubbing to watch this crusty yellow wonder pass. He passed right by the basin, heading straight for the green cubbyhole where his favorite sandwich was stashed and waiting, the crabmeat and raisin-bread sandwich I had made him.

Each morning for a month, Melvin, Bertrand, and I could be seen trudging homeward in the fuschia glow of dawn. With aching feet, carrying our rolled-up stinking aprons, exhausted beyond hope, we were greeted only by snarling dogs guarding their sleeping owners from this trio of odoriferous oddballs who came stumbling suddenly by their picket fences.

After nine, ten, or sometimes twelve hours of work, all we could think of was food, very briefly, then sleep. Filthy though we were, there was no energy left for baths—and no space anyway, since the moment we got home, all three aprons and six gloves were immediately tossed into the bathtub, where they lay soaking as we slept.

In the hot August afternoons we slept after a fashion, tossing and turning fitfully on roasting hot pillows in the sun, trying unsuccessfully to ignore the roar of semis coming through town on Main Street, groaning up from the lower valleys, in a seemingly never-ending stream, downshifting through traffic lights, loaded with corn, corn, and more corn. The sleeping subconscious could see it all: the enormity of the harvest pouring in from all the fields—the heaps of green things filling trucks in cob convoys like giant leaf-cutting insects; being dumped onto the blackened concrete of Twin City Foods, shoved ruthlessly by forklifts onto the first squeaking belt, then sucked into the hellish belly of the corn cathedral to be steamed, stripped of their green robes down to naked yellow kernels: sorted, frozen, packaged—all with such unbelievable noise and complexity, and all so that anybody's mother could stroll into Safeway and pick up a tiny package of frozen succotash for dinner.

One night, close to the end of the season, a six-foot-four ball player took LSD at the cannery. He followed me into the women's bathroom with pupils as large as Motown 45s. I came right out, but he stayed in. No one dared to go and see what he was doing in there, so Bertrand took the opportunity to exercise some of his pent-up aggressions—the ones he'd gotten in Northport, Long Island, where greasers used to beat him up, calling "Hey Goldilocks!" when his hair was long. Now he wore his hair just like those greasers who had inspired such hatred in him before, short and slicked back with a DA.

As it turned out, the football player wasn't pissing in the sink or squirting jism on the mirror—as everyone morbidly half-hoped he was. He was merely staring at the wall when Bertrand marched in. "Okay! C'mon—OUT!" he commanded brazenly in a New York cop's tone, ten times bigger than himself. The towering muscleman in a hairnet came padding docilely out behind Bertrand's skinny little authoritative being, and many women whose bladders were full to bursting breathed sighs of relief.

The corn season finally ground to a halt, and with the money saved from the cannery, Bertrand and I decided to go to Morocco. The only hitch was, we had just enough for one-way tickets—so our simple solution was to stay there *forever*. Melvin had his next year cut out for him, now that he could keep himself in Camels, Olympia beer, and jazz records. As Bertrand saw it, he and Melvin had been together constantly for four years and that was enough. They needed a break from each other. It was time for Melvin to hold his own for a change.

One Indian summer day in October of 1975, Bertrand and I took a walk out to Kittitas to see my mother and brother before we left on our journey to Morocco. My car Fred had long since capsized, so we were without wheels. But the prospect of a six-mile stroll was not at all distasteful, considering the good weather. And we were in no hurry. On and on our faithful feet took us on the straight old farm road, through flat fairy-tale valley scenes. It was the same road I'd driven that Halloween night a year before with the stereo when

I first met Melvin and Bertrand. We passed the Nanum Vue Dairy with its wonderful manure halo . . . *Funny how shit and milk kind of go together with cows, and yet it's still so natural and wholesome.* I dared not mention this thought to Bertrand, however, for fear he'd go into one of his "wholesome" fits.

We walked along in silence for quite some time, and then Bertrand began to talk.

"You know, I have an idea—a sort of a plan, you might call it."

"Yeah? What's that?" I perked up.

"Well, hmmm . . . you might think it's a silly idea."

"No, tell me. I'm sure it's not silly."

"Oh, I don't know. You'll probably laugh," he stalled.

"Come on, I promise I won't laugh!"

"Well, okay, here goes. We're going to Morocco, right?"

"Yeah, I hope so."

"To live there forever, right?"

"Yeah, so?" I was getting impatient.

"Well, my father said he would give me some silver bars—"

"He did?"

"—if and *when* I get *married.*" Bertrand winced.

"Oh, Bertrand! I don't think that's a silly idea at all."

"You don't?" He looked up cautiously.

"No, not at all. I think it's a *wonderful* plan!"

And so, we left Melvin in his little Dogtown house and my mother and David in the Kittitas shack, the cannery which was already retooling for carrots, and the flat October fields which were once again yawning in wait for snow. Having bought deliberately old-fashioned suitcases from a little secondhand store, we took the Canadian National train from Vancouver to Montreal. Bertrand had taken it a few years back and was disappointed to find it newer than he remembered. But snaking through the Canadian Rockies was exhilarating—the relentless Eastward clacketing motion just what we needed after a whole month in the cannery; and corn, corn, *corn*.

In Queens, at Bertrand's father's house we got married. It was a small, uproarious ceremony made even more entertaining by the presence of Bertrand's brother Gerard, who played best man and pretended to lose the ring. After drinking great quantities of gin and tonic, we made off with our old-fashioned suitcases, carrying the silver bars—and the deed was done.

We were both so young and irresponsible that the whole idea of getting married was nothing more than a lark, another in a series of adventures. And our reasoning to each other was simple enough: we were doing it for the silver bars.

9

Port Authority bus terminal in Manhattan teemed with the usual assortment of mixed nuts that morning. It was November 13, 1975. Suddenly, through the garish orange hallways came a couple of anachronistic characters, huffing and puffing up the spittle-ridden ramps with old-fashioned suitcases.

It was Mr. and Mrs. Halcott, newlyweds on their way to a honeymoon. She was slightly older than he, by about four years, though no one would have guessed; he was nineteen. She wore a calf-length skirt of dark blue with red pinstripes, a tan suede jacket, and old ladies' walking shoes, the kind with decorative holes tooled in and a thick two-inch heel. Oh yes, and stockings with a seam up the back.

Mr. Halcott had on a baggy pair of mustard-colored wool pants, suspenders which were visible whenever the chill soot wind of labyrinthine bus dungeons blew open his ill-fitting jacket for a moment, and to top it off, a Stetson gangster hat, half a size too big, which he kept pushing up on his forehead with a spare index so he could see. He carried a black alligator bag with pleats, while she lugged a square-cornered leather affair encircled by two belts. The great clock by the ceiling said 10:42. It beamed down its singular message like a sad full moon broadcasts its face of craters. The newlyweds craned their necks to look up at it, their pace quickening visibly—his one stride to two-and-a-half steps of hers.

"Hey buddy, can we borrow your sister?" A piercing shout rang out, echoing after them.

Mr. Halcott, a true New Yorker, didn't bat an eyelash, but kept right on track in spite of (or perhaps because of) the rush of adrenaline which now burned through his blood. Mrs. Halcott, also a native New Yorker, reacted in almost the same way, except for muttering "*fuckers*" between clenched teeth. This gave her an added boost, like jet propulsion, to keep pace with her new husband. The bus was scheduled to depart at 10:45. They now had two minutes left.

The Halcotts' strange attire, the speed with which they hurried, and the fact that they were bound for a totally different dimension made them prime targets for ridicule. They cut a striking apparition as they zoomed quickly through the horrific orange corridors, almost as if standing on a conveyor belt. It seemed that as long as they kept up speed they were safe from attackers—protected by a force field of sorts. And perhaps thanks to a hostile group of Times Square sleazeballs, they made the bus just in time.

10

The rainy dock in Camden, New Jersey, showed no sign of life. We stood huddled under an enormous gray umbrella, staring at our warped and rain-spotted reflections in filthy green water. Towering above us, the mammoth rust-streaked hull of the *Tuhobic* loomed quietly, and even higher up in the misty gray sky was its blue smokestack with bright red communist star, which without warning let fly a soul-shattering blast. Once on board the Yugoslavian freighter Bertrand wanted to go exploring when he realized that it was the very same boat he'd been on with Melvin years ago. I stayed below in the cabin, and first of all I pasted a small reproduction of Van Gogh's *Lemons* on the wooden wall next to my bunk. Then I lay down and stared into it until I drifted off to sleep, lulled by the hypnotic pitch and roll of the *Tuhobic*.

I dreamed about my mother and brother back in Kittitas. My mother had gotten a new brainstorm, a method of quitting both coffee and cigarettes at the same time: she was brewing her Bugler tobacco in the turquoise-enamel coffee pot. David took this as a sign that he should leave home, and over his bedroom he had rigged up a hot air balloon which was carefully designed to lift the roof off as it went. He was hurriedly loading all his *National Geographics*, foreign coins, and thunder eggs onto the tar paper while holding his nose with one hand and complaining bitterly about the tobacco stench. I was up on the roof with him and noticed a bum sleeping in burlap sacks, surrounded by empty bottles. I peeked in and saw that it was my *father*.

This discovery was truly magical—that wonderful joyous feeling that only a dream can bring. But David was mortified at this new development because it messed up his plans. Now he couldn't leave home after all. Down below, our mother was saying sarcastically, "Ahh, the prodigal father—I knew he'd return someday." I kept trying to wake him up, wondering at the same time, *Does this mean we'll all finally be together?* Then I looked again—and it was only Alphonso.

When I awoke, deeply troubled from the outcome of the dream, I had an intense desire to crawl back in and fix things, to make it right again, to bring back my father. The sky through the porthole looked much darker now. How long had I been sleeping? I ventured out on deck in search of Bertrand.

"Ah, there you are," we both said at once, as the strong wind blew us together. This made me happy . . . his coat . . . the smell of damp wool reminded me of the way my stepfather used to smell in Missouri when he would suddenly appear in the middle of a Brownie Scout meeting: full of awesome nighttime pheromones of an adult world.

But now here I was with Bertrand, my husband, a younger man. What sort of father was this? Did every man have to be a father? Maybe I could make him into a son. No, that didn't ring true somehow. I felt him pulling away, and realized I had been hanging on to the embrace longer than usual, smelling his coat and thinking these things. Some other passengers had appeared on deck, and Bertrand didn't want them to see.

Through the horrific industrial wastelands of New Jersey, the stately forests of smokestacks looming in graying yellow fog, we held our breath. Burnt coffee, dirty socks, rotten eggs, gasoline—it was an odorama to boggle the nose. This coastline, once so gentle and feathered with deciduous woods where the Iroquois and Algonquin padded on soft moccasin feet, this enchanted shore which so inspired Dutch painters only three short centuries before—what on earth had *happened?*

Soon we were out on the open sea of cobalt Atlantic, bounding along in buffeting salt spray, fast asleep hugging great Slavic pillows in cabin #13. And then, we weren't moving anymore—just the lapping sway of another harbor's filthy green waters. I got up to investigate.

Baltimore. Everyone was up on deck watching spellbound as rough tough longshoremen lowered forklifts into the ship's hold, a hole so exceedingly deep and dark, it was dizzying to behold.

The Yugo crew had reluctantly agreed to let the Baltimore dockworkers operate their winches, but they looked worried. There was a good deal of shouting as gigantic logs were dragged out of the gaping hold, first by forklifts, then secured with cable and hoisted up. The bark of these logs emitted a wonderful sagey fragrance. It was being rubbed off by all the friction and twisting. Were these some exotic Old World timbers imported from Baltic forests?

They succeeded in getting one of the monstrous trunks up from below and onto the dock. And another. But the third one was not a charm—it came swaying and twirling unsteadily, making a wide eccentric arc as the winch operator struggled to control it. Everyone ducked as it swung low over our heads—and then, as if in slow motion, it crashed like a battering ram into an ornate wooden railing— SMABASH! All hell broke loose. The Yugoslavian crew began screaming unintelligible curses at the longshoremen, and the Baltimorian thugs revealed the full extent of their moxie. The captain of the *Tuhobic* came out, livid, holding a blue document which he thumped rhythmically.

"*Dambums*—hurt my ship! I make you pay!" he roared. All the passengers retreated to safety—except me and Bertrand, so fascinated were we by all this madness. Not the type of spectacle we could witness every day.

The intruders left, and soon a Yugo sailor came out on deck with glue and sandpaper and a little bucket of shellac to repair the smashed railing. As he lovingly worked, a peach sunset behind him, he periodically mumbled Serbo-Croatian curses to himself and glowered in the direction of Baltimore.

Paralleling the scrubby dunes of the Eastern Seaboard, we were clipping right along through calm waters that evening. A bell was ringing somewhere down in the labyrinths of the ship. Its insistent tinkling sound taunted my ears through the steady southern wind. The bell finally came to fetch me, held in the hand of a cook in food-white.

"Come, dinnertime," he pronounced with Slavic persuasiveness. I followed him obediently into the gullet of the *Tuhobic*, past all the Swiss international signs, through narrow esophageal hallways to the second-class dining room where a long table was set with delightfully misspelled name placards at each place. All the other passengers were there already. I was the only straggler.

I slipped into my empty waiting chair next to "Mr. Hallcort" and noticed the soup bowls: ponderous thick white china with thin blue bands and distinctive anchors of the same deep blue around the rims. The tablecloth was soft, padded like an ironing board, and the bowls sank heavily into it like steam irons.

These perceptions of heaviness, softness, and density flung me into deep infantile reveries, rekindling a sensation I used to have during high fevers in early childhood which I called *The Crunchy*

Dream, in which sounds were always greatly magnified and lingering, and my fingertips felt as dense as dwarf stars.

Our towering waiter, Dinko, was ladling soup from the tureen . . . I was mesmerized by the amber liquid swirling into my bowl. Someone was nudging my arm.

"Hey, wake up, what's wrong with you?" Mr. Hallcort whispered anxiously at me.

Someone turned up the stereo and lights, and everything wheeled back into sharp focus. . . . *The bounding motion of the boat, and this marvel of a man who did the soup ballet, a six-foot-four Atlas with such incredible grace and balance who hefted great platters of shifting liquids in the middle of a shifting liquid sea . . .*

"Yes, sorry, I'm okay now—tell you later." I squeezed Bertrand's hand under the ironing board and smiled what I hoped was a reassuring smile.

All the passengers fell to, slurping soup self-consciously, and now it reminded me of Bellevue's psycho ward . . . those women in ill-fitting bathrobes, eating with clumsy spoons that said PROPERTY OF THE CITY OF NEW YORK to remind us where we were, in case we hadn't already noticed. . . . But these blue anchors were far more inspiring—and no one here was on Thorazine.

Dinko was back now, weight lifting the second course, an unrecognizable mixture of brown stuff. I asked him what it was, hoping to learn about some exotic tidbit of Yugoslavian cuisine. But all he said was, "PEASBEANSMEAT—GOOD! EAT!"

We were all destined to become very familiar with this dish in the next three weeks, as was the entire sewer system of the *Tuhobic.*

In the morning, before the breakfast bell had even dreamed of tinkling, I was up in the prow playing figurehead, the sun rising over the Atlantic warming my back. We were heading west now, through a seemingly endless stretch of green clumps. A saltwater swamp. The ship plowed on within a narrow waterway cordoned off by buoys. Strange dark hulks approached us, going the other way, some with Sanskrit squiggles, others piled high with cars from Japan, all of them looking decidedly alien and deserted. Then a row of colonial buildings appeared to my left, brightly sun-smeared and mirroring the water out of which they sprouted—various shades of brick, bright as oil paints on an expressionist's canvas.

This was Savannah, Georgia. And along with all the other passengers, we were ordered to walk the gangplank for mandatory infestation of the town that afternoon. Bertrand and I discovered a beautiful park which upon closer inspection turned out to be the yellow fever cemetery. We sat on a bench for a few hours, wondering about a strong odor of earwax which was all-pervasive around the gravestones. At Woolworth's we shared an old-fashioned peach cobbler at a Twilight Zone soda fountain from the thirties and bought some black plastic deck shoes for me.

The beach at Jacksonville, Florida, was our last chance to sink feet into sand—last touch of land before three weeks of Atlantic crossing. Next land, if we ever saw any, would be Africa. Trudging gratefully, breathlessly over the dunes, we turned to look back at the freighter—our *mother*, docked this time on a sandbar in the middle of nowhere, awaiting our return.

We thought it was a mirage at first—the shimmering blobs of red far away—but as we got closer, instead of dissolving the blobs seemed to separate into distinct red objects. These rhomboid hulks were none other than English double-decker buses, the kind they have in London. What were they doing here on this windy sandswept beach in Florida? Some were lying on their sides; all of them were rusted, deserted. Probably dumped by some other freighter years ago.

This sandbox came equipped with an amusement park—lifesized toys for us to play in! We clambered into one of the oven-hot buses. Bertrand claimed the driver's seat and began yanking the arthritic steering wheel around.

"Allo luv! C'mon up! That's awroit, you can roid fer free if yer wi' me."

I immediately bumped my head on a MIND YOUR HEAD sign, and then tried out the toasty seats in their varying degrees of springiness and dehydration.

"Looka this! Some bloke's left 'is paypah," I called to the driver, who played along: "Let's 'ave a look." It was a *Sun* scandal sheet, a sort of British version of *The National Enquirer* from 1965. Ten years old, all crisp and yellowed and full of sand. The two of us sat in the roasting old bus guffawing over the crumbling articles, reading them aloud to each other in phony Cockney accents like a couple of bloody fools until we nearly passed out from the heat. It was a splendidly ironic farewell to the Western Hemisphere.

11

Strolling in my plastic Savannah deck shoes over salty green paint one afternoon, a hand touched my shoulder—Bertrand? No, this wasn't like him; he'd more likely announce his approach from far away. This was the guy who sat across from me at dinner—Max.

I gasped in genuine surprise. Max held a frayed, much-read paperback in one hand. He seemed in fact to be hiding it behind his back, but he wasn't sure whether or not to hide it.

"Recognize this?" he asked suddenly, revealing the cover which I eyed with playful suspicion. A photo, all in bronze tints, of my father in a cowboy hat.

"Yes, I've heard of that one."

"*Heard* of it! Haven't you read it?" Max's incredulity verged on annoyance.

"No, but I'd like to—"

"God! I thought you'd have read *all* of his books!"

We stood there, teetering on the edge of something. . . . His strong expectations about my father were unformed, so he wanted something from *me*, wanted me to confirm something about my father for him. But he didn't know what it was and neither did I. I could feel his expectation and resented it. After all, how could I possibly give him any part of my father—when I'd only met him twice!?

"Well, you can keep the book. See ya at dinner!" Gazing down into the churning wake of pistachio froth, I wondered at my own sadness. Even to me it was obscure. So strange how tears could appear right in the middle of a thought or sentence, for no apparent reason. It almost seemed that one of those curly wavelets down below was the cause of my tears. How could a little wave make me so sad?

Ah, but I was trying to trick myself. Really I knew it was my father—the little pang of memory that he had ignored me all those years. Not a *wave*. The pinpoint of pain had touched my heart just as I was staring into the water. *My God. This is like surgery*. I sighed deeply. The sore spot in my chest slowly dissolved now, and I hoped the sea wind would cool my eyes quickly.

Impulsively, I opened the paperback Max had left me to a random page and read

SLOBS OF THE KITCHEN SEA

The title of a chapter. I read on, amazed. It was all about my father's own experience on a Yugoslavian freighter.

Somewhere in the mid-Atlantic mid-November midnight a door was rattling. I climbed out of my berth and wandered down the hall with a matchbook to stuff into the offending doorjamb. The source of the noise, however, turned out to be the door of the boiler room itself. A dark man was climbing up the greasy metal stairs, emerging from the complexities of the ship's rumbling abdomen. Evidently the head mechanic, he took me on a gestured tour of the boiler room without a word of English. Afterward, he invited me into his tiny cabin way below the water level for a drink of Yugoslavian plum brandy—slivovitz. The man from the boiler room was taking the plum lace strap gently down from my shoulder. *How sweet of him,* I thought, through a plum haze. *So natural to be down here in the true heart of the* Tuhobic *with the only man who knew all of its workings.* Here in the interior the pummeling was soothing, all-pervasive—not the shallow strident rattling that had roused me from my bed. We fell together in the heave of ocean swells and soft sensuality of plum fire. . . . Then I was staggering through the maze of corridors looking for cabin #13 and Bertrand. Back in bed I passed out and dreamed I was lost in the ship and the purple lace of my gown got caught in the greasy railings and I slipped and slid and all the cabin doors had the same number. I opened one door and popped right out on deck. There was Dinko in the moonlight, his hair blowing wildly in the wind, tossing huge loads of garbage into the sea. I watched, aghast, and noticed after a while that it consisted mostly of bright blue cracker boxes. I squinted at the bright yellow letters, trying to make out the Yugoslavian brand name. They all said

KÊRÖUÁÇZK

I was awakened by Bertrand at the porthole yelling "Land ho!" We were approaching a far-off misty whale of sand—a behemoth of a dune—*Africa.*

12

Casablanca. Daytime chaos of dust and taxis . . . The naive American consciousness had perhaps expected something more romantic? A shadowy visage of Bogart in a fedora and young Bergman crying on a rainy runway at night, uncanny piano tinkling from nowhere. These glamorous celluloid illusions kept themselves brutally camouflaged, however, hidden beneath layers of time and concrete.

I stood stunned on the dry North African dirt, gazing up in bewilderment at sturdy, salt-bashed *Tuhobic*. I'd been expelled from my mother's womb prematurely. Dumped THUD onto land before I could walk. I felt about as balanced as a gimballed pool table.

Dizzily we made our way to the "bus station"—a far cry from Port Authority. A disorderly mob of figures in striped robes shouted and tossed bundles back and forth. In the center of all this commotion was something resembling a bus, but there was no way to squeeze through the crowd to it. Bertrand made a valiant effort to barge ahead, grabbing my hand tightly and cursing under his breath. But before we could reach the full-to-bursting vehicle it took off in a cloud of black fumes and ear-splitting unmuffled fart blasts. The vacant rectangle where the bus had stood quickly filled in with people, and we found ourselves stuck in a human hurricane. There was nothing to do but sit down on our bags and laugh. For nearly half an hour we entertained ourselves by watching all the shoes go by.

Observing the gamut of footwear milling about, we came to the conclusion that by far the most common were pointed open-heeled slippers à la Ali Baba, though toned down for modern times. Next in line came biblical sandals with crisscrossing leather straps, then Western businessman shoes, a few high heels peeking out from under the robes of precocious veiled housewives, and on down the spectrum to the rag-wrapped, and lastly unwrapped, foot.

A whole day of waiting and shuffling and sweating and rumbling in stuffy buses was what it took to get from Casablanca to Essaouira. But at the end, we nonetheless hopped out onto the nighttime cobblestones with renewed enthusiasm.

"Okay, as I remember, this is the street that leads to Mahmudi's house." Bertrand began walking briskly down a dark alleyway, and I followed close behind. I knew exactly how he must feel returning to old beloved territory after so long, unannounced and unexpected. Similar, I thought, to the way I had felt coming back from South America to my mother's shack in Kittitas. . . .

Over the dark cobblestones I ran, following Bertrand in his mad radar race toward Mahmudi's house. Soon, I was sure, all the rushing would be over and we would be sitting on Moroccan rugs in soft lamplight around a *tagine* of couscous and lamb, lulled by hashish and guttural Arabic. Bertrand and I would become Moroccans. I would go with Sadiya into the casbah wearing a veil, something I'd always longed to do, to buy spices and dyes and pots, to learn to handle durham and bargain—all the secrets of a woman's life—

while Bertrand ran off with the other men to drink mint tea in cafés and commune with Allah in the mosques.

These visions were superimposed over Bertrand's fast-moving heels, visions of our new life unfurling before me in imagined Technicolor. The synchronized sounds of oud and tabla were so clear in my mind's ear that I didn't hear anyone approach—

"Don't look now, but we've got company! Just stick close to me." I could sense that Bertrand's lost-in-the-Bronx-subways-at-3-AM adrenalin was pumping. Behind us and advancing quickly was a large crowd of small boys. We were being escorted through the streets of Essaouira by thirty tough street urchins. Not only were they tough, they were slick, clever, desperate, and trilingual to boot.

"Monsieur, Madame, we carry your bags for you?"

"Come. We show you a nice hotel—the best." Now they had skipped ahead and were surrounding us in a Muslim crescent formation, trying to "carry" Bertrand's suitcase—coincidentally the one with the silver bars inside.

"Getthefuckouttaheah!" He swung the suitcase in a wide arc, letting them know he was serious, and they retreated momentarily— but, like flies, came right back.

We had a purpose, a destination, as in Port Authority a month before. But now we had only one card left in our hand—Mahmudi's place. And this card loomed so large, had grown to such mammoth proportions, so much was bet on it, that it was hard to see it as one card. *Sanctuary*—the blue door! We were nearing it now, urchins in hot pursuit. It was an arched wooden door like all the others, very high and painted bright Moroccan blue—

"This is it," panted Bertrand. We rushed forward with such single-minded fervor that we didn't even see the padlock until the last moment. We couldn't believe our eyes. Bertrand grabbed it to make sure he wasn't hallucinating, then slammed the heavy metal against the blue wood as if it were a doorknocker. Mahmudi's sanctuary was no more. There we were, backed up against the door like a couple of cornered rats, unable to collect our thoughts. Heads spinning with ifs and whys and maybes, we turned and burst through the vulturish mob—Monsieur et Madame swallowed their pride and had no choice but to settle for "a nice hotel" that night.

In the following days, we tried to find out what had happened to Mahmudi, but no one wanted to talk. It was rainy and unseasonably cold for Morocco, and we shivered in our cool dungeonlike hotel room which was designed for roasting hot weather. Finally, after we'd hung around in a number of cafés by the drizzly beach, an old man who remembered Bertrand from before told him that Mahmudi had been arrested for hashish dealing a few years ago. He might as well have told us that Mahmudi was dead.

It was a hard blow for Bertrand, to know that he would probably never see his friend again, but he soon got over it as other considerations such as warmth and shelter vied for first place. When he first got the idea, I could have sworn I saw a light bulb switching on in his head, like in a cartoon. "England! We'll go to England!" he declared, jumping up from his chair. "They have electric heaters there, and brick houses, and—"

"And I can write my book, and we can drink tea—"

"I have some other friends we can visit up there, and at least we could get *warm*."

This new obsession brought us together with shared intensity. Now we had a fresh goal in common.

So it was back to Casablanca again. And from Casablanca another northbound bus, to Tangier . . . a photo flashed in my mind—my father, shirtless and smiling on a beach—a black and white photo I'd seen in some book somewhere. . . . It said *Tangier, 1957.* I wondered what he had been doing there, the year my twin sisters were born. Then I saw my mother on the steps of New York Hospital, hugely pregnant under a cashmere coat. . . .

CRASH BASH BUMP. Djellaba-clad figures were loading five

lambs onto the roof of the bus and sliding others down into a sea of rough hands and baskets. At first, on the trip down, the treatment of the lambs had disturbed me to the point of tears, but now I began to think that the lambs' plight was no worse than the humans', packed as we were into the suffocating interior. Perhaps the roof was the preferred way to travel after all.

Gazing out at the mosques of unearthly white that dotted the Atlas mountains like surrealistic pearls—so pure and shadowless that they seemed to lack all dimension—I became aware of an annoying pressure. It was in my bladder.

"Bertrand, guess what? I have to *pee*." I turned to him with a look of tentative terror.

"Oh great! Good luck!" He took off his hat and held it upside down by my feet. "Here, milady, pray pee in this."

"Please don't make me laugh—oh no!" I laughed, crossing my legs tightly in desperation. I busied myself for the next ten miles with intense urethral concentration, wondering how on earth the Arabs manage to never urinate for fifteen-hour stretches on these hellish bus journeys. Did they have some built-in metabolic capacity to store moisture, like camels in the desert?

Just as I was beginning to seriously consider the alternative of peeing on the floor in a secret stream, which I would carefully engineer to flow through a rusted hole in the floor, we came to an abrupt lurching halt in a decidedly nowhereish place.

A few women clambered out with some small children. Even the driver got out to kick the tires and spit on them. I followed the other deserters and was literally relieved to find we were all of the same mind. Behind a clump of bushes we micturated in unison over cacti. No toilet paper, but no matter—I'd given up on that stuff days ago.

"Ahh, the simple pleasures," I sighed, returning to my seat. "I'll take that any day over an Arab toilet."

13

In Tangier we sat at a rickety table on the dirt, a raggedy canvas awning overhead, picking at fish bones in the middle of a dusty square. For hours and hours we had been waiting for our baggage, which had been tied to the roof of another bus. Bertrand ran his fingers through his hair and cursed under his breath about the silver bars and how you could never trust the Arabs. I fed scraps of fish to tough alleycats and wondered if I would ever see my manuscript again. We swatted flies with a vengeance on the checkered plastic tablecloth. Hooded characters periodically slithered over to our table, trying to con us out of the baggage claim ticket, saying that they knew where the suitcases were. But Bertrand wasn't falling for that.

We had almost given up hope when lo and behold, a top-heavy vehicle roared into the plaza like a hot-rod garbage truck, loaded with bags, bundles, and more live lambs. We both jumped up (a little too quickly, making it obvious that there was something of value in the suitcases). Even with the matching claim ticket it was a struggle to get the bags: the man in charge just shook his head "no," which exasperated Bertrand no end. I was afraid he'd have apoplexy. But his rage finally worked, and we got the bags. And by then it was too late to catch the ferry across Gibraltar, so we climbed into a waiting taxi. When the driver turned around, it was like a *One Step Beyond* TV nightmare—he was one of the sleazos who had tried to get the baggage claim ticket from us earlier. He drove us in circles, all over the city, up high where we could see the whole town below, and finally to a hotel with chairs all piled up outside. Several figures were coming toward the cab as he pulled up—our ordeal wasn't over yet. Bertrand put a knife to the driver's neck and whispered, *"Drive,* you motherfucker."

His New York bravado had really come through for us this time. I was truly impressed. That night in our pink hotel room with its flimsy cardboard walls, we slept lightly, wondering what they imagined was in our suitcases.

In the morning, underlit by the glare of sand, Bertrand and I stood by the door of the ferry office, inquiring about timetables and where to buy tickets.

"*A que hora sale el transbordador para Algeciras?*" I asked the Spanish Arab in charge.

"*Sale a la una y media,*" he answered, looking directly at Bertrand, who understood not a word of Spanish.

This was interesting

"*Y, por favor, donde podemos comprar los boletos?*"

He did it again—not even acknowledging my existence.

"*Alla, cerca del coche negro, ve?*" He pointed to a black car from Bertrand's vantage point. I figured that this must be a certain brand of masculine pride, fraternal honor, for this Arab (the very word itself means *man*) to recognize only other men. He didn't want Bertrand to feel embarrassed, so I was serving merely as a ventriloquist.

As this strangely lopsided conversation wore on, I was surprised to find it *refreshing* to be so totally ignored. In all the places I'd lived or traveled—New York, Mexico, South America—men had always been either overly attentive toward women or had displayed a certain empty imbecilic chivalry typical of Christian society. But this treatment was truly novel. I had always dreamed of being able to make myself invisible, and now this Spanish Arab was doing it for me. How ironic—invisible but not silent. Perhaps here the old adage was reversed? Women should be heard but not seen.

I couldn't help but think of all the women I knew back in the States who would be infuriated under these circumstances. So, what's different about me? Why do I enjoy this?

At first the question was perplexing, but soon an answer began to pour over my head like lemon sauce over warm gingerbread. *I need to be ignored because it reminds me of my father.* Yes, that was it. My father's lack of interest was the only attention I'd ever gotten from him. Now I needed *more.* How backward! How odd to crave indifference from men. And for some obscure reason this new discovery made me happy.

The ferry across the Strait of Gibraltar to Algeciras was far rougher than our transatlantic freighter ride had been. We stood, bracing ourselves in the prow under a glassed-in section over which waves were crashing as the small boat dipped and floundered. Behind us, on rows of orange seats and on the floor, were sad heaps of Moroccans—veiled moaning figures sniffing lemons and praying. A desert people who were definitely not in their element.

HEEBRALTAHRR

The Spanish pronunciation of Gibraltar. I repeated the word as an incantation as we crashed through the waves. It seemed to appease the spirit of the strait and ward off queasiness—for me, anyway.

That night on the strangely deserted Costa del Sol, we were

served by what must have been the shyest waiter in the world. He was very young. And apparently so fearful of eye contact—he somehow managed to tuck his whole face behind his arm while painfully placing stewed whole tomatoes on our plates—that we thought surely he'd turn his neck inside-out. He was so shy that we didn't even dare laugh at him—and that, for us, was unusual.

14

Through Gatwick's mad rush of civilized confusion we expatriate refugees now fled, fumbling frantically with heavy unfamiliar coinage at the alien pay phones, looking lost on towering escalators, getting caught in turnstiles and holding up vexed commuters in the mayhem of Victoria, then out onto desolate gray railway platforms in the bone-chilling mist. Where on earth were we going?

Boarding a red double-decker bus, we had a mutual déja vù under a MIND YOUR HEAD sign, and it all became clear. Those mirages on the sandy bosom of North America three weeks ago were more than a playground. They were an omen, a foreshadowing of what was to come. We had thought we were going to Morocco, but they knew better. They had even set the mood, which was one of giddy playfulness, as we stumbled across traffic roundabouts, were nearly run over by lorries, fed pigeons next to old men in front of the British

Museum, and raced through the Underground, forgetting our tickets on the way out and getting scolded by fatherly conductors.

After a few nights at the Gloucester Road Youth Hostel, we went in search of Bertrand's friends who, unlike Mahmudi, still existed. In Thornton Heath at Ike and Jackie's flat, the merriment continued, as the Scottish lass and her West Indian boyfriend delighted at the novelty of having such "crazy Americans" staying with them. Jackie was especially tickled by Bertrand's exaggerated Newyorkese—and I felt I was witnessing a replay of the Halloween party where I'd met Bertrand in Dogtown. Our unlikely foursome hit all the best pubs, drinking pints of Guinness and throwing darts. We stayed with them in their little flat overlooking Grange Park—had hangovers together and tea together and all scrambled desperately for shillings when the gas heater started pluffing and threatening to go out. Then they went to Scotland for Christmas vacation and left us to care for the place and the two birds, an African whydah and a canary.

As soon as Bertrand and I were alone, doubts began to surface in our relationship, like bubbles in a swamp. No more audience. The uproarious nonstop banter having ceased, we were left with only ourselves once again, and so we retreated into separate hermit crab shells. It seemed that the only time we truly clicked was when there was an enlivening factor of some sort, an outside influence—whether entertaining or catastrophic didn't matter. Now that everything had simmered down to a dial tone, we both felt powerless to make any waves in the swamp . . . just these bubbles of doubt.

I busied myself with the birds, feeding them figs turned inside-out and stuck to the bars of their cage. I loved to hear the sound of their beaks snapping the tiny seeds. Then one day I discovered little trays of fresh sprouts at the greengrocer's. What were they? "Rapeseed, luv, rapeseed. *Rapeseed*," said the greengrocer's wife in a shrill, birdlike voice. She seemed quite enamored of the name. I stopped feeding the birds rapeseed sprouts when they started making ear-shattering screeches and green splats began to spew from between the rungs and onto the carpet. When their bird-bellies were back to normal, I let them out to roam the flat. They made excellent rug cleaners, pecking up crumbs one by one.

Money from the silver bars, our wedding present, was running out. By January we had found a bed-sitter right next to Ike and Jackie's flat at 41 Grange Park Road. Bertrand's attempts to get working papers had been unsuccessful, and with all the money gone, we resorted to a new pastime—stealing milk bottles. This was one thing we did together, refueling a certain kinship that was temporarily lost during the uneventful spell of ease. Out in the harsh gray mists in oversized secondhand wool coats we'd huddle, scooping up bottles from the steps (only one from each family), silver caps for regular and gold for extra rich—a full three inches of yellow butterfat extending down the neck. Yes, those bottles of milk, Typhoo tea (the pick-me-up cuppa), and McVittie's digestive biscuits comprised our entire food intake that winter.

In our bed-sitter we had an electric heater, the kind with silly fake glowing coals at the bottom. Bertrand had put the finishing touch on it, though, when he cut a photo of a large green lizard out of *Life* magazine and pasted it on the metal plate of the heater. Now it looked as though a giant dinosaur was rearing up from prehistoric volcanoes. It was better than a TV set, and I often found myself staring catatonically into it while searching for a word or phrase to tap out on Jackie's asteriskless typewriter.

At the tail end of our stay in London, Bertrand got into the habit of spending a lot of time in his favorite pub on the corner, while I sat inside all cozy and warm with the lizard heater, writing about Costa Rica on the old British Royal and listening to armies of mice running up and down in the bricked-in fireplace.

15

City of beginnings . . . city of constant flux . . . port of filth. Our very own city. Best and worst in the world. City of rot, rigidity, dark beauty, horrible wonder, and plain pain. Once again we were feeling the same thing, though neither of us knew it, communication having dimmed—gone opaque like Pernod to which water has been added.

It was the sensation of a foot slipping into an old, well-worn shoe that was left in a cool, dark closet and all but forgotten until now—and the surprise at discovering that it still fits so well, even though the foot has changed, has worn so many other tight and ill-fitting shoes. Old flesh and old leather greet each other like long-lost brethren, embrace, meld.

The concrete contours of our old, well-worn city now folded around us smoothly. Slick black grime in the pavement greeted us like a welcome mat. The City, a multispiked magnet, was reclaiming two of its own, two more stray metal shavings. We were tired, and so was New York tired, but the weariness of New York was so great, the disintegration so all-encompassing, that somehow this made the city even stronger.

All the rot and filth and soot and garbage and sewage and spit saturating every crack in the granite structure seemed to glue it together, imitating the tar. In fact, anything that isn't concrete, stone, or steel on this marvel of an island eventually becomes tar. Pigeons, rats, seaweed, cockroaches, mango peels, bottle caps—all TAR.

Prodigal rats returning to a sinking ship, we looked much the same as we had at the very start of the journey, three months earlier in Port Authority, only now we hurried through hellbound tunnels to Jamaica, Queens.

On the F train, with its rattly horrific soot-windows sealed forever with crud more ancient than Egyptian tombs, its graffiti-ravaged walls, gum-dotted floor, and flickering lights, we sat opposite each other and saw the failure written in our eyes. Ever since we'd met, we'd built the trip abroad into such a mountainous molehill that this homecoming was a major letdown. And yet, each of us felt secretly relieved. Relieved to be enveloped once more in the Known, however shabby. This was easier than plunging headlong into a glittering, exotic Unknown.

On the last stretch, the shadowy green underbelly of the el in Queens, we walked in a strange dreamscape of echoing footsteps. Two Puerto Rican women looked us up and down with intense scrutiny and then one remarked to the other, "OOOoooooooooooh, safari . . . safaaaaaari." They nodded in agreement—must have noticed the faded pink stickers, which still clung to our bags, bearing the word TANGIER.

16

Bertrand's brother Gerard was, like him, a comedian. But a very different breed of humor ran helter-skelter through his veins. For, whereas Bertrand was the younger of the two and could make an utter mess of his life and still be forgiven by his father, Gerard was under pressure to succeed. He had somehow developed a TV "game show host" attitude which he used as an effective carapace to avoid anything unpleasant.

I got the feeling while talking to him that he was sequestered somewhere far inside a fortress, and that if his innermost self were to be probed or punctured, Gerard might die from the shock.

Sensing this (and it may have been all my imagination), I found it fascinatingly paradoxical to talk to him. I felt I had a similar shell, though not nearly as thick. Bantering with Gerard's outer self was highly entertaining for me, kind of like playing hide-and-seek with a hermit crab, a challenge I could enjoy almost any time of the day or night now, since the three of us lived in the same apartment.

Even his guitar playing (and he did it fantastically) seemed to be a parody of guitar playing, his whole life a parody of itself. And yet, there was something substantial about Gerard, something sweet and intriguing. And I was afraid to get too close, for fear of falling in love with him. *My husband's brother . . .* that would never do!

I would call "Anyone for tea?" The answer was invariably "Me!" By the time I had carried their grandmother's flowery blue cups and saucers into the living room, the Scrabble, Monopoly, or Risk board was already set up on the coffee table, the evening in full swing.

It was hard to say how it got started, but in a short time the three of us became thoroughly attached to "tea and games."

Gerard was the MC, the DJ, the fount of trivial knowledge, and the catalyst without whom nothing could have happened. Bertrand and I were both thankful for his enlivening presence, twisted and superficial though it was, because it delayed our having to come to terms with our own dimming affaire.

On one of these cozy evenings, after we'd all recovered from the horrors of subway commuting, Bertrand had an idea: Why not do everything at once: Risk, Scrabble, Monopoly, Poker, Clue—and watch TV!? So we tried it. It was a frenetic race round and round the table.

"Okay, let's see—it's my turn at Scrabble; your turn at cards, Bert (Gerard was the only one who could get away with calling him by this nickname); and, madame, your turn at Clue."

"Hey, is parridy a word?"

"Wait a minute, two aces don't beat a royal flush!"

"It's P-A-R-O-D-Y. Look it up if you don't believe me."

"Mrs. Peacock in the billiard room with the icicle—"

"Watch out now, I've got three continents—"

"All right, you jokers, I'm buying Park Place."

"What? You can't roll twice—I saw that!"

"Attick attack attick attackin' Japan!"

"Whose turn *is* it?"

"Sure, I'll have some more tea."

"Your deal, Mrs. Halcott."

"But I want to watch *The Untouchables*. The ad's over."

"No, this is a triple *word* score, count it!"

"Well, *I* think it's Mr. Pink in the boudoir with the meat grinder. . . ."

"There is no meat grinder, what're you talkin' about?"

"Okay, just wanted to see if you were still awake. I mean the wrench."

"Blackjack is more fun."

"Jesus! This could take all night!"

"Yeah, let's just watch TV."

"Not till I take over the world—that's not fair!"

"Well, anyway, you can't yet, 'cause I'm on Kamchatka."

"Hold everything—*The Honeymooners* is on!"

We were like kids whose parents had left the house one day and never returned. And for me it was a real treat to be the only girl with two brothers, having grown up in a matriarchy.

The honeycomb pattern in the black-and-white marble tile floor of the bathroom in Queens played tricks on my eyes and my mind, flashing me back to a brownstone building of my infancy: 200 West Sixty-eighth Street at Amsterdam Avenue, a place long since buried in the prehistoric rubble of Manhattan.

Languishing in the sturdy clawfoot tub, I combed the tangles from my thoughts. During extensive ablutions, desperately needed to counterbalance the forty-five minutes of subway commuting each day, I got into the habit of talking to my reflection in the misty mirror, trying different accents until I hit on one that my other self responded to. The British Nanny was my favorite . . .

"My dear girl, what on earth do you think you're doing?"

"Well." (The answer came in the form of a younger rebellious

American tone.) "What's it look like I'm doing? Taking a bath fer Christ's sake!"

But the real answer was always silent, under water—inside a towel. . . .

╾╾╾ ╾╾╾ ╾╾╾ ╾╾╾ Funny you should ask. I'm living with my second husband and his brother avoiding the issue biding my time far from my mother and brother the only family I have left in this world except for two lost twin half-sisters and John, my first husband and oldest friend. So what am I doing taking a bath as the planet spins why doesn't all the water fly out of the tub and where oh where is my father everyone else seems to have a father why not me? And John is far away too . . . must write John can't talk to Bertrand why did we get married anyway because of the silver bars or to live in Morocco forever am I stupid?

And why am I writing about these crazy things I did in Peru? Who the hell cares? Maybe I do—maybe I have to, have to write about it all so it will disperse like blood in the ocean or like ink staining a blotter through my hands and feet my ears my eyes dripping underground to petrify and become stone engravings for people to read because I didn't bring a camera and no one else can see the Rio Perené and the banana trees and the canoe maybe a painting would be better certainly would be more fun than sitting here like this twisting my spine into driftwood hour after hour maybe I'll die at the typewriter and they'll find a skeleton hunched over with metacarpal bones resting on the keys THE END.

Why? Did there have to be a reason? I liked to think that reasons weren't needed at all. I'd always been fond of the notion that things just happened like cards falling or dice clicketing from the random hands of Fate. It was easier that way—no responsibility. And with no dependents, responsibility seemed rather unnecessary. If I had brought up the baby . . . if Natasha had been a live birth, what then? Then I would have an eight-year-old daughter, and I probably would never have gone to South America, so I couldn't write about it.

Suddenly I understood, or thought I understood, my father's predicament way back in 1951, when he had looked askance at my pregnant mother from his rolls of teletype paper on West 10th Street and said, "Hey, I can't take care of a kid. I gotta write this book!"

Books and babies—cabbages and kings—sealing wax on Daddy Jack's magic babblings—of, of, of . . .

17

On Bertrand's birthday, a chill night toward the end of March, we all breezed into the city to hear Chico Hamilton at the Village Gate. In the amber maroon glow of jazz and booze each of us got drunk very fast and reverted to adolescent behavior patterns. Bertrand slipped back into his panhandling persona, to prove to himself that he could still pull it off. I danced and writhed like a deranged coquette, believing myself to be the same "Lolita" that Henry Cru had accused me of being at the age of twelve on nearby MacDougal Street. And Gerard became Basically Bad, reeling unscathed past impossibly dangerous situations, insulting uninsultable thugs and somehow getting away with it.

After a timeless spell of Chico's wild voodoo rhythm, I had a sudden urge to see my old neighborhood and started to stagger in the general direction of the East River. Bertrand and Gerard followed, duty bound to protect me. Lunging past battered trash cans and marching along in the heady New York sewer breeze was invigorating. Fortunately, by the time we reached the corner of Sixth Street and Avenue C we had sobered up somewhat. I had just pinpointed my old stoop down the shadowy block, 709 East Sixth Street, and was considering actually going in—to get a chip of paint or some such poignant souvenir for my mother, when a shout rang out—"HEY, AL CAPONE!"—followed closely by a bottle which shattered at our feet. The shout and accompanying bottle both originated from my precious old address, the stoop of which, on closer inspection, seemed to have sprouted a menacing clump of mushroomesque heads: Afros silhouetted against a bluish street lamp.

Our adrenals switched into high gear then, and we booked our three paddy asses on up to the dubious safety of Fourteenth Street, dimly aware that it had been Bertrand's hat they were referring to. Oh well, a bottle cap dug from the Precambrian tar of Second Avenue would have to do—or, better yet, a manhole cover! What a great addition to David's coin collection that would make!

On a bus uptown, threading the deserted canyonlands of 3 AM Manhattan, the three of us sat in the rear section of a lurching rhombus, shades on, trying to ignore the fluorescent glare. We sat separately, Gerard in the extreme right rear blowing cigarette smoke out the window, Bertrand in the extreme left rear, and me in front of him at the next window. A nondescript middle-aged Caucasian man sat on the aisle. He'd been there for quite a few blocks, sitting silently, when without warning he bellowed, "PUT OUT THAT CIGARETTE!"

We all ignored him, hoping he was just some luny venting steam. But then he repeated it louder, and it became clear that he was aiming it at Gerard.

"What cigarette?" Gerard said in a belligerent yodel, waving both hands to show that they were empty after flicking the evidence out the window. The man got up and approached Gerard; and like a knee-jerk reflex, both Bertrand and I jumped up too—jack-in-the-box bodyguards. The vigilante, unaware until then that we were all together, suddenly feeling outnumbered, wheeled around. "All right you goddamned kids!"

But it was too late, my fists were already sunk into his work shirt and I was pushing him with pure, unadulterated hatred—the *idea* that anyone would try to harm my beloved *Gerard* made my blood boil. I was a miniature locomotive, plowing into the chest of the intruder

BWONNNNNNNG

I slumped dizzily onto a plastic seat. The vigilante had backhanded me in the face, and the bus jerked to a halt. Everyone was yelling.

"Out, *out!* Take your fight off the bus! Jesus, there's never a cop around when you need one!" The black bus driver was half-directing his complaints to a bag lady who sat up front. Bertrand was hurling obscenities and threats at my attacker while raining him with karate kicks and punches, Gerard was trying to restrain his brother—and the old vet just stood there unfazed, solid as a boulder.

He hopped off the bus at Ninety-first Street and Third Avenue, Bertrand at his heels like a crazed jackal chasing a weary lion. Gerard and I reluctantly trailed, already purged of anger.

"Sonofabitch—you hit my wife—I'll kill you!" Bertrand shrieked ineffectually at the tough old coot, whose sole objective now seemed to be to get home and hide. He was making a bee line for some projects by the East River. Bertrand paused to dig some bottles out of a trash can and hurl them at his prey. It was oddly refreshing to be the aggressor for a change—but a pathetically transparent mimicry, considering what had happened downtown earlier the same night. I could hardly keep up, and Gerard was only hoping his mad brother would fail to catch the sturdy old Mick since, if he succeeded, Bertrand would most likely be made into corned beef hash. Bertrand probably knew this too, but since the chase was already under way, he figured he'd milk it for all the drama it was worth. At last—it was over and the birthday boy pounded desperately on a closing elevator door instead of on flesh. We turned him away, calming him, bound for the subways and the return home to 179th Street, Jamaica . . . the end of the line.

We had all taken turns protecting each other from real and imaginary foes, and yet we still had enough energy left to leap over yellow turnstiles like freshly minted juvenile delinquents—to race into a humming open train and swing on the greasy chrome posts as if they were maypoles, in a sudden resurgence of sheer city hyperactivity.

The scenes going on in these cars made the daytime commute look like a country hayride. In the first bubble a long-haired blond kid lay on the seats all bloody; the gang of hoods who had just mugged him were just leaving, skittering through the cars like psychotic cockroaches. Bertrand, realizing that he might have been that kid if things had worked out differently, went over to him and asked, "Hey, man, you all right? Need a doctor?"

"Just leave me alone, mothafuckah!" The kid yelled blindly, too delirious to reason.

We switched cars at this point (the old man just getting on probably thought *we* were the ones who mugged the kid), only to find a madwoman doing a striptease and muttering to herself. This deeply offended some black youths with a boom box. We decided a whole new train was in order—only to run into a man threatening his girlfriend with a gun, while, three cars away, some cops were prodding a Chinese bum with billy clubs.

Gerard took this opportunity to bellow as we were exiting the dungeons, "Hey! Don't you dumb fuzz have anything better to do? Why dontcha go three cars up and help that girl who *needs* help?"

After this 4 AM subway nightmare I found myself fondly reminiscing about the gentle weirdos of the rush hour: that huge fat man with waxen skin covered in red bites who carried an assortment of plastic gallon jugs with him, tubes originating from somewhere within the voluminous folds of his coat, dripping and oozing unimaginable brown substance—*he* never had any trouble finding an empty seat, or three, or five, as high-heeled secretaries and murderous maniacs alike cringingly gave him a wide berth.

Ah yes, and there was the strange little man in mismatched plaids who frantically ran his fingers through his thinning hair like tarantulas whenever the train stopped at a station. And I could not forget the dark disturbed Iranian who always rode between cars in the morning, staring down at the tracks and repeating, "Rat shit! It's all rat shit. . . . That's all it is—RAT SHIT."

Sunday dinner at Pritchard's was, as usual, the shining cherry atop the whole Dairy Queen dung heap of the week. Pritchard was a seventy-three-year-old scholar of Greek history and philosophy, and the boyfriend of Bertrand and Gerard's sixty-seven-year-old grandmother. The reason we three could live in her old apartment was that she had gone to live with Pritchard, several blocks away in the Victorian house he was born in. It stood out quite conspicuously in the block, this well-preserved relic in the midst of newer ramshackle dwellings on 171st Street. Pritchard and Juliana even slept in the same iron-runged bed he was born in. Pritchard had been a bachelor all his life until "Gram" appeared, and since it was most definitely *his* house, he was the one who called the shots, and she just had to put up with his eccentric bachelor life-style.

Pritchard did everything wrong—delightfully wrong. He washed dishes with Ajax cleanser and left them sitting in the sink all covered with gritty blue swirls. He made instant coffee with half a cup of instant granules to half a cup of hot tap water—and then boiled the resulting black syrup before drinking it down with relish. He took cold baths and often slept with his clothes on, he opened cans with a church key and kept them in the refrigerator opened with all the jagged edges sticking out. He never did any physical exercise, but drove his '74 Cordoba at ninety miles an hour. And despite it all,

Pritchard seemed to be in perfect health. He had all his own teeth and a thick head of white hair and the blood pressure of an athlete—and somehow he managed to walk unscathed through the streets of the ghettos, even though he was a perfect target for muggers.

Besides our beloved ritual of tea and games at the apartment, Gerard, Bertrand, and I had also gotten quite attached to the ritual of Sunday dinner at Pritchard's. There in the ornate sitting room, unchanged since the twenties, we could languish in plush chairs with clinking cocktails while helping Pritchard do the *New York Times* crossword puzzle in the roast-redolent atmosphere emanating from Juliana's kitchen doings. It was the perfect way to unwind and recuperate from the week-long stress of jobs and subway commuting.

But on the Sunday after Bertrand's birthday, we were all so hung over that we passed up the predinner cocktails. Pritchard was in his upstairs study rummaging through some ancient dusty volumes (his favorite pastime) when I went up looking for some aspirin for my head.

"Uhh, hello, hello, . . ." he said in a voice that could only be described as Jimmy Stewartesque. Then he took me by surprise, squeezing my ass and trying to kiss me.

"Aw, c'mon honey, c'mon . . ." just as Gram was yelling from below, "Pwritchaaaaad! Dinner's ready!"

"No, please, Pritchard. Don't. We have to go downstairs."

Sunday dinner was rather strained that week: the two brothers had no appetite, Pritchard was trying to feel me up under the tablecloth, and Gram had burned the lamb.

"Aaah, the Ides of March are upon us, my friends. But never fear, soon it will be April, the foolest month," pronounced Pritchard in a Shakespearean tone to the solemn dinner table, chuckling to himself and carving the charred carcass ever so slowly like a giant benevolent, white-haired snail.

"Strange . . . I thought that was something I invented," I mused, putting mint jelly on my peas.

18

The train jerked madly from side to side through flooded stretches of Nebraska. I sat in the dining car alone, jerking along with the train and trying to drink a gin and tonic. The train trip was a neutral spell, like the *Tuhobic* voyage had been, during which time one gathered one's wits—in the hope that one would be ready for the station and the stationary world when the train stopped. This time I would be ready.

King Street Station in Seattle seemed anything but stationary, but I felt ready enough. Into the monumental ladies room I strode, carrying the same old suitcase I'd been carrying for months but with a few more rips and belts added. Bertrand was waiting outside.

One moment all was solid and secure and definite—and then I looked in the mirror, at the same moment catching a whiff of some strange fruity fragrance. What was it? Something from childhood . . . like *strawberry Kool-Aid*. The sight of my own face which I knew so well, lit by garish yellow sink bulbs, and this oddly festive smell combined with the general murmured echo of the whole vaulted station—and everything turned inside out: an unearthly rumbling vortex sucked me into another dimension; I took a deep breath—what was going on? I felt totally alien, and yet it was as though this alien feeling was something that had stayed away for a long time, an old familiar feeling of superstrangeness, returning to reassure me: "Yes, you are most definitely strange and alien after all." The reassuring part was that everything else seemed equally strange in the same familiar way—a uniform substance like warm custard pouring into my senses. Am I going insane? Savoring this possibility, I left the ladies room, completely forgetting what I had come in to do, and reentered into the great megamurmur of a thousand voices, rain outside, gray mist—I was light as air and the mist beckoned, requesting my presence in it. The whiff of strawberry Kool-Aid had long since been usurped by old leather, perfume, piss, disinfectant, cigarette smoke, and rainy streets—in that order.

"JAN!" A funny boyish man in old man's clothing was calling to me. "What took you so long?"

Wait a minute. Do I know him? I turned around to look more closely at his face, fragments of a story tickling my memory. There was a sense of having done something wrong, missed the point. The boyish man was painfully familiar, almost like a brother—*but I really shouldn't talk to strangers*. So I just said, "Oh, hi." And kept going.

"Well, what the hell did you do with the suitcase?" He was following me. I tried to appear cognizant, stalling in the hope that things would clarify. "The suitcase," I parroted, as it all played back in reverse slow motion. . . .

"Yeah. This is Bertrand, your hubby, remember me?"

His sarcasm came to the rescue and I almost thanked him, catching myself just in time.

Staying in the back of a friend's antique store in Tacoma, we felt a little like refugees from Nowhere. And the drizzly weather only added to our depression. At Boysenberry Antiques there was not much to do but listen to jets droning overhead and scrutinize the help wanted classifieds. We both found jobs quickly, but Bertrand's was a minimum wage dishwashing job, whereas mine was assistant cook at the Tacoma Ritz Hotel.

The cook I assisted was a white boy from Oklahoma named Bruce who emanated blackness from every pore. This quirk alone would have been enough to entice me, since at that point I craved some soulful spice in my life. But there were other things about him too—a deep voice, a commanding presence, a jovial disposition. . . .

Up on the twelfth floor of the Ritz, working closely together under stress every night in the intense heat from grills and broilers was creating a bond. We were being fused with perspiration and grease splatters. I had noticed something about kitchen work that was amazingly conducive to romance: put two people of the opposite sex in a kitchen and get them cooking, and—as long as the germ of attraction was already there—BINGO, instant chemistry. I had seen it happen many times in a number of restaurants in Santa Fe five years earlier. That was before I met Bertrand—even before I'd been to South America.

And now, here it was all over again—that luny food madness in the air. A brand-new Ma and Pa team, thrown together in such fitting circumstances. Bending over to retrieve a fallen baked potato, in the heat of the moment, Bruce would offhandedly slap my derriere, which was clad in black and white checkered pants the same as his. Both of us wore chef's hats, though he preferred his straight up, while I flattened mine like a mushroom. The homogeneous uniform of cookdom camouflaged the difference of our sex, making the prospect of uncovering it later all the more fascinating.

When "later" finally came (we got the inevitable drinks gratis from the bartender), instead of a long, dreary bus ride across town to Bertrand at the Boysenberry, I went with Bruce to a gay bar on the waterfront. There, we got our second, third, and fourth winds of the evening, dancing and carrying on (it was the short-lived era of the hustle), drinking like fish into the wee hours. He drove me home, and after a lascivious goodnight feel, I found myself creeping into the back of the antique shop at 5 AM. I lay in bed beside Bertrand, feeling stifled, the wild events of the evening still flickering in my vision. We were tiring of each other's company, and I was beyond the point of no return . . . having tasted the poison. He had already lost me.

Night after night at the Ritz, the magnetic pull between Bruce and me intensified.

Punching the clock, peeling off food-splattered aprons, getting free drinks—it was closing time again, and the sickly smell of grill cleaner filled the air of the shiny kitchen which we knew was really filthy underneath.

"Hey, babe. C'mere, I got an idea."

I followed Bruce down a red-carpeted hallway, clinking White Russian in hand.

"Ooooh. Where are you taking me?"

"I know just the place, cream puff."

"Are we sneaking into the pool?"

"Better'n that, I got the keys to this room, babe, right here."

"But are you sure—"

"*Hey*, don't worry 'bout a thing. You're with *me*, arentcha?"

"Oh boy, I can take a shower!"

"*We* can take a shower," he corrected, as I pulverized the last of my ice between my teeth. We both shed our grungy cook's clothes and stepped over pristine pink tile to the shower. Warm and damp, our clean bodies exuded fresh sweat on the crisp hotel sheets and each other. We tumbled across the inviting tundra of a king-sized bed, lit only by multihued flashes from the TV.

Bruce was big, around six feet—a real bruiser. His face was smoothly handsome except for a scar on his jaw, which only added to the appeal. I had been longing for a larger man—larger in stature, and presence, and . . . —who could make me feel petite and feminine by comparison. With this great big bear of a man I felt like twinkle-toes, a wispy vixen held firmly in his arms. Safe. Protected.

With my first paycheck, I rented an apartment on Pine Street. I told Bertrand after the fact and gave a flippant offhand explanation to the folks back home at the antique shop: "Well, I can't be taking long bus rides in the dark after work every night!" In the past month my relationship with Bertrand had dwindled to a mere annoyance. The humor and clowning had long since gone out of our affaire, and we had begun snapping at each other. So I made a clean break.

And Bruce, it just so happened, also needed a place close to work, so we wound up sharing the place on Pine Street.

When my burly new roommate saw all my old secondhand clothes, he flipped. "Hey, baby, throw these rags away! We're gonna get you a whole new wardrobe."

"But I *love* this. And this. Can't I keep some of them?"

I never stopped to think what his motives might be, believing in my gullible way that he had my best interests at heart. It was a dangerously bad habit, confusing sex with love. And while part of me knew it was dangerous, I wasn't quite ready to admit it. That would mean derailing, completely going off the circular toy track of a comfortable syndrome with men. It would be difficult, painful. Therefore it could wait.

My Oklahoma fry-cook had a plan for making a lot of money *real fast*. He had done it before, so he knew it was foolproof. I was all ears.

"Well, it's simple. You just open a joint checking account for Mr. and Mrs. Halcott and put in, say, twenty-five dollars."

"That's *all*?"

"*First* thing you do is go out and buy some really spiffy threads, honey. Like for you I'd say a silk blouse, beige cashmere coat, Italian leather pumps, and *most* important, a gold Cross pen."

"Why the pen?" My brow was furrowed.

"So you can look really *legit* and reek of good breeding when you put your John Hancock on those kites, baby."

There was a viscous silence in the apartment, as these ideas were slowly processed.

"It's nothing but strategy, babe. All you got backing you up is your attitude."

Strategy. I remembered that very same word being used by a shoplifting buddy back in New York to describe the way he had waltzed out of a supermarket with a quart of milk in his hand in front of all the checkers, looking perfectly unruffled, grinning, believing it was okay—believing so strongly that everyone else believed it too.

"Like 'The Emperor's New Clothes,' " I said at length.

"*Exactly.*"

Bruce fit right into a certain gangster image, fulfilling a fantasy I'd been dreaming up ever since age seven. Suspenders were a large part of this fantasy . . . crisscrossed over a shirt that enclosed a large masculine back. Shadowy afternoon ambience contributed immensely to the lustful mood. Like naptime with Peter Bunks in Wappingers Falls: I was being a very bad girl—doing very naughty things with a very bad boy, and loving every minute of it.

The day the printed checks arrived, Bruce insisted that I throw out all of my old clothes. It was all part of the plan, he said. I took him literally and tossed them out the window into an alley, where, at least I figured, some scavenger like my former self could make use of them. Out they flew into the rainy Tacoma night, and I was filled with an odd mixture of sadness and elation.

Returning home from the liquor store with daiquiri makings, we were greeted by an unusual spectacle: one whole side of the rough brick four-story building was plastered with my old clothes. The sea wind had blown them back, and now they clung in surrealistic poses to its surface: pants all stretched out, as though scaling the wall, brassieres and sweaters trying to climb in someone's window. They glowed eerily in the darkness, like the work of a giant prankster. Laughing our way up the stairs, we caught our breath and proceeded to "daiquirize" in celebration of the check scam.

Someone was knocking on the door. I answered it—and there was Bertrand in the hall, looking smaller than ever. Seeing him sobered me somewhat.

"I've come to say good-bye," he pronounced darkly under his perennial fedora. Pulling the overcoat snugly around himself, he added, "I'm going back to New York."

"Oh, really . . . you are?" I was at a loss for words, and dared not invite him in. *Had he seen the clothes?*

"Who's that, baby?" came the booming voice from within the apartment, explaining everything. These two men were so vastly different that it scared me. The idea that they might meet was unthinkable—it would be hate at first sight. I knew what Bertrand would say about Bruce: "What a dumb fuckin' oaf!" And if Bruce saw Bertrand, his response would surely be "Who is that weasly little twirp, baby?"

Bertrand handed me a crumpled address and turned away.

"I'll write you. Good luck!" I called after him, feeling quite guilty, wondering what was going on in Bertrand's mind. And wondering, too, what sort of twisted lapidary had cut my facets, so that I refracted such polar opposites.

"Come on back in here, babe!" For the first time then, I heard something in Bruce's tone that rubbed my fur the wrong way. But I couldn't put my paw on it.

19

The week began with dead serious theatrics. A sedate-looking Bonnie and Clyde hit all the major downtown department stores, not to mention countless ritzy boutiques. Not only did we both get new wardrobes, we also played the "returned gift" game (this was where the cold cash came in). The easiest mark for this was Pendleton shirts.

I would waltz into a store (after a crash course from Bruce)—redolent of L'Air du Temps, fit to kill, "legit" down to the last molecule of my Capezio heels, well mannered yet haughty—and say, "Oh yes, and I'd like them gift wrapped."

Next day I'd return, toting a rustling cargo of bags from many stores—obviously a bountiful shopper—and with a slightly distraught air, produce from the demolished mass of tissue and ribbon a plaid shirt:

"He didn't like the color." Or "This didn't fit." And "Yes, I'd like a refund please." It was fun practicing the dry, irreproachable tone of a wealthy inconvenienced customer, a role I'd never been cast in before.

"Cash or charge?"

"Oh, cash," I would answer belatedly, distracted from some more indulgent browsing: "And do you carry these in taupe?" A handful of such runs would net several hundred smackeroos.

Sometimes Bruce would come with me, posing as Mr. Halcott, and the two of us at once were thoroughly intimidating. He had the dense aura of a plainclothes cop, and a knack for switching without warning from a contagious clean-cut Midwestern laugh to a menacing twitch of the eye and jaw which made many a salesgirl fear for her job.

Back at the apartment on Pine Street, we partners in crime counted our loot on the bed: twenty-seven hundred. Not bad for one week of "shopping." It was doing my self-image good to have all these new clothes. Never in my life had I owned a real leather jacket or a cashmere coat, except for secondhand versions from the Salvation Army. I began to wonder if crime *did* pay.

One week had passed.

"Okay, it's time to tear up the paper," I announced, following Bruce's original foolproof instructions to a T.

"But baby, we forgot to get you a hat! We gotta make just one more run."

"They'll have us on the computer by now," I objected.

"Hey, trust me. It'll be okay, you'll see."

I balked and argued—but in the end he persuaded me with his soft-sell salesman rap, and off we went.

That evening an impeccably dressed couple were chauffeured in handcuffs to the police station.

"Just let me do the talking, babe," Bruce whispered in my ear in the back seat.

"Foolproof, huh?" I said, shaking my head in disgust. Inside the station, I couldn't believe the bravado of this con-man cook. Now he was bullying the *cops*, acting as indignant as an enraged elephant. They were having a hell of a time restraining him. And it seemed that every time they were on the verge of marshalling extra men (it took six to hold him), he'd calm down and confuse them with extremely gentlemanly behavior.

Meanwhile, I struggled through interrogation and papers, trying to give out as little information as possible until I knew what Bruce was up to, so that our stories would jibe. It was like walking a tightrope blindfolded. Despite it all I still had to spend the night in the clinker with some tough black women and white-trash floozies. The cell reminded me of the juvenile detention home in The Bronx where I'd spent four months of my adolescence, only this was far worse. I surprised myself that night by praying—something I hadn't done since Christmas in Peru during the earthquake. And now under a gray wool blanket on the hard bunk by a pink cinder-block wall, I realized what a stupid thing it had been to get involved with Bruce's check scam.

A clinking of keys reached my ears after a seemingly endless spell of blank, dark nothingness . . . and I awoke to the apparition of a warden opening up the bars. Miraculously, he picked *me*. And so, in wrinkled cashmere reeking of cigarette smoke, I went through a hurried court session and got out on P.R. Not public relations, not Puerto Rican, but personal recognizance.

"What did you do?" I asked Bruce in the blessedly fresh free air of a Tacoma bus stop.

His aptitude as a con man, it seemed, had really come through for us. All night long, as I had writhed in nightmares by a graffiti-covered wall, Bruce had been carrying on a constant dialogue with the police chief, talking circles around him. A deal was made whereby Bruce would lead them to a big heroin dealer in exchange for our freedom.

I was so grateful to be out of that hellhole, but something inside me cringed at the thought of finking on anyone. Back in the mid-sixties in the New York drug scene, I remembered, to be a fink was to sink to the lowest rung in the universe. So by all accounts I should have been relieved to discover that Bruce had no intention of keeping his half of the bargain.

"Start packin', babe, we're blowin' this pop stand!"

What a conniver . . . always two-and-a-half steps ahead, I mused, secretly stuffing some of my old clothes from the alleyway into a brand spanking-new Samsonite.

20

Up and down Portland's wet quadrated streets . . . it was sweet freedom to wander in the rain like this with a big white umbrella, past bakeries, bookstores, orange bus stops. I was wearing my ill-gotten leather jacket made in Turkey, gray wool pants, and graceful boots with sturdy heels so that I could crunch along the same way my mother used to on New York sidewalks when I was but a babe. That was it—Portland reminded me of New York! That is, one tiny neighborhood in uptown Manhattan, like somewhere around Broadway and the upper seventies.

Walking aimlessly in the cold rain wasn't nearly so bad when you were dressed for it. . . . So, here I am, a well-dressed felon, a warrant out for my arrest—laying low from the law—probably wind up in prison someday. . . . But why dwell on the future? Right then, the present moment was much more interesting.

I rounded a corner, and there was that odd, Twilight Zone restaurant I liked so much, Archie's. The name as well as the lettering on the sign fascinated me for some reason. It was kind of art deco in a shabby old way, like a sewing pattern from the thirties which had been left in a sunny window to fade: still sleek of line, though out of style. I approached the glass door of Archie's, all wrapped up in these soothing ruminations and feeling as I imagined my mother might have felt in her modeling days.

"Hey, mama!" came a loud shout from somewhere, shattering my mood and irritating the hell out of me. Then whistles and sucking noises like Puerto Rican hoods used to make from slum hallways. I spun around in a fast fit of fury and flipped them off, noticing that they were on the first floor of the Grand Hotel across the street— the hotel where I was staying with Bruce. Three guys out on a ledge with nothing better to do than yell catcalls at passing women. I was so mad, I gave them the whole arm FUCK YOU before whirling into my favorite café in Portland with the air of an enraged Indian goddess. Not serenely, as I had planned my entrance to be. Originally I had wanted to sit by the window, but now that those assholes had made that impossible, I stole away to a dark booth to try and regain my previous composure.

Performing the strangely supernatural feat of "relaxing with a cup of coffee," I pondered my anger: most of my life so far, the prevailing winds of emotion had been joy, sadness, fear, indifference. Irritation was usually the closest I came to anger. Oh, *except* for that time in Kittitas when the little redneck boy beat up David. But usually so far my anger was directed at males only. Women scared me. Men I felt I had some control over—some kind of leverage. The thought of violent confrontation with a woman always cowed me, flashing me back to the loony bins and detention homes of New York where I'd been beaten up by women and girls.

Half an hour and three cups of mediocre coffee later, I felt sufficiently fortified to exit Archie's. Stepping gingerly out the plate-glass door, my glance up at the hotel windows was purely automatic. But now, in place of a few horny obnoxious fellows was the un-mistakable muzzle of a rifle—aimed directly at me. Beyond its tubular protuberance all was dark. There was only the black rectangle of the window with the stark metal circle in the center—and a dull gleam of terror.

My shock flung me bodily back into the safety of Archie's door-way. Flattened me against the wall with thudding heart. So, I made them *that mad*. I was amazed, more than anything, at the lightning-fast computing my mind had done at the mere sight of the darkened window with the little circle in the middle—really nothing more than an abstract graphics piece. Well, I would have to be more careful with this anger if it was to have such a powerful effect on men. Deserted—why? Had they put the rifle up there just to scare me, or were they really crazy enough to snipe from a second-story hotel window at a woman emerging from a restaurant in broad daylight? It was pointless to conjecture. I picked a wild random second to slip away, fairly shaking with adrenaline, making a mental note of which room they must be in by the number of windows from our room—and ran into the very same hotel.

When I told Bruce about the incident, he wasted no time in getting up, jaw muscle throbbing in a display of machismo, and swaggering down to the identified room.

"You're *sure* this is the one," he said to me, almost threateningly, before knocking. I nodded. He was in his undershirt, muscles bared.

"What's this I hear about someone pointin' a piece at my old lady?" he growled, face twitching dangerously, cracking his knuckles. I stayed around the corner in the hallway, but near enough not to miss anything. I recognized the guy who came to the door, and the voices from within sounded meek and guilty.

"Uh, what? I don't know. Not me—not *us*."

It was a rare treat to be "protected" like this: I was so accustomed to simply running and hiding from dangerous situations. But this seemed even more frightening somehow.

Bruce and I stayed in Portland all February and March of 1977, cooking in different restaurants, yet managing to avoid any new kitchen romances. But one May morning in the bright airy apartment we had rented, in the pale lemon yellow kitchen where just the night before I had made fried breaded sole, and Bruce had bestowed upon me that wonderful compliment, "Honey, you cook fish like niggers cook fish!" there was a knock at the door. I sat lazily at the table in my bathrobe while Bruce answered it. Some friend of his whom I had never met was there. I listened groggily to their macho dealings in the hallway, still feeling a pleasant tingling soreness from his thrustings the previous night. I stretched and smiled to myself, wondering if all men who were good lovers had to be so crude.

Bruce swaggered into the kitchen and his friend waited in the living room, barely visible.

"I'm goin' out for a while with Barry, babe—so clean up this pigsty, huh?" This was unusual. He had never ordered me to clean up any of our pigsties before.

"I'll clean it up later. Right now I've got to write," I said, drying my hands on a dish towel hanging on the refrigerator door. Unexpectedly he snatched the towel and lowered his voice to a loud whisper through clenched teeth:

"Goddamnit! You better clean up this place right away, 'cause I don't want to see it like this when I get back, you hear?" He slapped me in the face with the towel for emphasis and left quickly.

"C'mon, Barry, let's go!"

I stood in the middle of the kitchen, stunned, though not hurt, nodding my head for a long time.

Yeah . . . okay . . . so you want to impress your buddy. . . . *Okay*. The rage built up inside slowly like a volcano. It was exhilarating. I became a hurricane, whirling madly through the place, carrying on an imaginary argument with the absentee Lord of the

Pigsty. . . . *Castle? Palace of Shit! All right, you macho fool, you want to see it clean? Then clean it yourself! Lick up this ratshit yourself, asshole, 'cause I'm leaving—I'm gone. Long* gone.

I whipped myself up into a healthy pneumatic frenzy, collecting all my things and throwing them into a suitcase, realizing what a perfectly typical "leaving home" scene it was. I had no money—so, what else was new? I knew how to get money, didn't I? Hundreds of ways to get *money*—illegal, fast, foolproof—in a pinch! And I'd done most of them, hadn't I? Yessiree Bob. My jaded alter ego was growing by leaps and bounds, fed by the furious fuel from this angry fire.

Yeah, I'll survive. How do you think I got this far? I can turn a trick, buy and sell some dope, steal something and hock it. Or, better yet . . . Best of all, Bruce baby, I can do just like you taught me to do.

In less than eight hours, a normal working day, I somehow managed to amass over four hundred dollars in a veritable blur of wrapping paper and Pendleton shirts. Precisely the way Bruce had shown me in Tacoma. But all the while knowing that I could absolutely not afford to be caught now, with a felony warrant hanging over my head. It would mean instant prison. My *chi* was abnormally strong that day. I felt superhuman. I stole shirts, stole *all* the wrapping paper, wrapped up the "presents" in alleyways, took them back without sales slips. And since I wasn't dressed nearly so spiffily as I had been during the check scam, I had to muster every available drop of *strategy*.

Miraculously, though, it all went like clockwork. It was May 31, 1977—the deadline, it so happened, to buy Greyhound bus tickets at a very low price. I sat on the bus, still in Portland, struggling with a sudden wave of remorse and indecision, imagining Bruce's reaction to my note—and my absence. I was just considering jumping up and forgetting the whole thing—on the teetering verge of leaving the bus and sharing the rest of the money with him: Surprise!

False ending, joke's on you . . . tumble into bed—when the bus decided for me, fuming out of the station with me and my suitcase firmly ensconced in the front seat.

Twenty-seven hours later, after a rollicking lurch southward through mysterious nighttime terrain of orange and pink glowing forest fires and unbelievably down-home truck stops, the unreal starburst heads of palm trees began to materialize beyond the smudged bus window, and twilight breathed its lavender sigh of relief into an exhausted soul.

21

The demon ear-spires of the Methodist church on Franklin Avenue in Hollywood must have been eavesdropping. We had been talking about the medieval regularity of their bells, how one could easily become programmed by the intervals of the chimings, when, as if on cue, they sounded a head-clearing reveille that bounced off the natural amphitheater of semitropical canyons in deeply resonant tones.

John, and I sat on a downward-sloping brick patio which seemed ready to spill into Franklin Avenue and the church at any moment. I brushed away the ants that were crawling across my bare feet, then ran into the house to rescue a hysterically screaming tea kettle. A few minutes later, as John cut the avocados, I noticed how well we still moved together in the tiny kitchen: with as much ease and harmony as we had done in New York, Yelapa, or Kittitas.

"What do you think? Should we remarry?"

"Why not? Taylor and Burton did."

Back out on the sloping patio with the ants and the lemon tree and the ever-blooming oleanders and the smog and the church spires, I picked a small greenish lemon for the tea. A few blossoms fell into my hand along with it, which I threw into the brew for good measure.

The exotic shrubbery surrounding us was steeping us in a special flavor of nostalgia. We both sat cross-legged on deck chairs, feet safe from ants, munching avocado-smeared muffins in the sun.

"Remember those limes we had in Yelapa?" I was referring to the coastal jungle where John and I had lived ten years before, after we escaped from New York when I was fifteen and pregnant.

"Mmmmm, yeah. You used to make whole pitchers of limeade in that chipped white enamel thing," John said with his mouth full.

"And the mosquito net. My *God*, do you realize we slept under that thing every single night for four months?"

"Yeah, and not for mosquitos, either."

I shuddered and shook my red kimono in exaggerated neurosis.

"Well, sweet, there are no scorpions to worry about here." My heart sang to hear him use this old endearment. I thought of all we had been through together—the Methedrine freaks in hallways on Avenue B, the attack by deranged soccer players in Guadalajara, federales, bats, the stillbirth in the jungle, nightmare trains across the Sonora desert, John carrying me because I couldn't walk. No matter how long, how many years we were apart, the magic of our connection always resumed itself flawlessly, without missing a beat, whenever we were reunited. John was and always would be the most important man in my life.

Almost every day since I'd come to Hollywood a letter appeared in the mailbox from Bruce. He wrote such moving chronicles of his heartbreak, the emptiness that filled his life since I had left— and all of them on the typewriter he had so generously stolen for me to write my book on. He admitted to being a stubborn pushy bastard and said he had learned a lot. He sent snapshots of himself looking so handsome and forlorn, signed with great scrawling brown Pentel—smudged, no doubt, with tears.

Each time I read one of these letters I was plunged into a fit of vacillation. I called him in Portland on John's phone, and the sound of his voice further confused me. The idea that this big burly hunk of a guy could cry for little me really fractured my sympathy bone.

Luckily, John happened by one day when I was reading Bruce's sixth letter, my foundations badly shaken.

"What are you reading, sweet?" John queried with a pickling glare from his green eyes.

"Oh, a letter . . . from someone." I sniffled.

"Someone, huh? Mind telling me who?" John's head was wobbling sideways to signify annoyance.

"Bruce," I admitted reluctantly.

"You look a bit gray around the gills there, my friend. Something bothering you?"

"Oh—I don't know. . . . I think I'll have to go back to him."

"Have to, hmmm? Go back, eh?" he said in a near whisper.

"Well, he's really sorry, and I—really do like him, and . . ."

"You don't sound very convinced. What's wrong, did the con man lose his knack for conning?" This was a full-voiced barb.

"Well, I already promised to go back. He's sending me a ticket and everything." Once again I felt the pressure of being caught between polar opposites, with no density of my own.

"Why do you *do* this to yourself?" he yelled, startling me.

"What do you mean?"

"This is your life, your *will*. I'll be really disappointed in you if you go back. Coming down here was one of the strongest, smartest moves I've seen you make." His green eyes drilled holes in my blue ones.

"Oh no. . . . I can't change my mind *again*. I don't know. . . ."

"Listen. That guy Bruce is an ASSHOLE. You yourself told me that. Got a soft spot in your heart for assholes? Better think about it." John got up abruptly to leave. He was grinning at me as he rolled down Sycamore in neutral.

"*You know* . . . ," he called from the window of his old white Jag with a crooked smile full of crazy wisdom.

I thought about it. In the house, all alone, lying on the blue carpet, by the red telephone; out on the brick ant patio with the oleanders and limes and earth tremors and the chiming Methodist church bells. And I found I did know.

One scintillating June morning in the lush desert dreamland, I went for a stroll on the hill. John was gone, staying at his current lady friend's mansion on Laurel Canyon, and I was left to my own devices. The glamorous astrality of Hollywood was coaxing forth an old wayward personality which I'd kept in mothballs for the past five years. I discovered a lovely Japanese garden, and climbing over bridges and fences with tiny spotlights, I arrived in the back of the Yamashiro Restaurant right next door to 2018 Sycamore, my humble hillside hideaway.

In a white string bikini, I strode through the back door of the swanky lounge and ordered a ginger ale, draping my towel over the stool and sitting on it. It wasn't very long before several men began conversations and offered to buy me drinks. And then, it seemed, before I knew it, I had been invited to a nearby hilltop house to swim in a pool.

Ahh . . . so here I was, only two weeks after the greyhound grind, reclining in the Southern Californian haze, sipping a clinking cranberry and Stolichnaya, pleasantly plotched, splashing in glimmering turquoise H_2O, already turning a smooth bronze under banana oil, with the whole L.A. skyline at my toes. Later, when the hills became a dark sequined evening dress, I found myself in a helicopter reeling away from ocean cliffs toward Catalina Island with a mysterious and fascinating Latin gentleman. I was being wined and dined in the most flamboyant style. Did I deserve all this? If I had played my cards just a little differently, I'd be rotting away in Walla Walla State Penitentiary right now. This adventure was just what I needed to reinforce the belief that I was capable of doing whatever—even magic, if I so willed.

There's a city down there under the cotton-ball haze this morning. I can hear it. I can feel it. Even through the riotous greenery of the canyon. Nothing to be sad about, no cause for any uneasiness now, in the heart of this life-sized glamour heap.

I still think of Bruce sometimes: poor soft brute up north somewhere, probably sitting around in overbleached jockey shorts, petting his white rats, wondering what happened. No. More likely he's shadow boxing in front of a full-length mirror, twitching his jaw and muttering, "Aw, you handsome motherfucker!"

The wonderful thing is, I don't *care* what he's doing. A few glimpses creep in occasionally for amusement, or perhaps it's morbid curiosity. But that's as far as it goes.

Writing . . . gazing into the greenery . . . contemplating the lemon blossoms . . . enjoying the edge of solitude. This is it. I feel the earth tremble and watch the ants day after day. The bittersweet choke of longing for companionship is a tonic now, a dull ache to be savored and not assuaged by fatuous seeking out of bar-room strangers or one-night stands. All the glittering possibilities of recognition and fabulous night life are within easy reach if I want them, but this is the hunger strike in the middle of the supermarket for me. Ironically the same experience John had for three years cradled here in this Hollywood hovel.

But during this spell of idyllic contemplation, I sorely needed a balance—something like a paperweight to hold me down to earth, keep me in touch with tactile solid reality. So naturally, when I saw the ad in the paper for a ceramics worker, I knew my void had been filled. For the whole year that followed, I would descend steep

Camrose Drive every morning on foot, past jade trees, figs, and palms, then take the bus down Cahuenga past NBC Studio, where there was always a line of people waiting to get into *The Tonight Show*, and finally arrive at the Burbank factory. There I'd make clay face pots with several other young women in a very laid back atmosphere, smoking grass and listening to Bowie and Eno. In the afternoons, when I'd return to my tiny sanctuary nestled in cliffside verdure, I'd wash off all the clay dust, rehydrate with cocoa butter lotion, and sit down at the typewriter. For a good half hour then, myriad cartoonish faces of my own invention danced before me, superimposed on whatever I was writing . . . scenes from the Arizona desert . . . LSD trips with Paul . . . massage parlors . . .

22

In September I was offered a job as an extra in *Heartbeat*, a movie about my father's ménage à trois with the Cassadys. One smog-laden morn, John drove me down to the shoot on Fourth Street. The Acropolis Café was just the place for a beat generation coffeehouse scene: a Greek restaurant in downtown L.A., unchanged since the thirties, its bare green walls easily took on the ambience of San Francisco in 1956.

In the wardrobe trailer, I sat right next to Nick Nolte, who was having his face expertly plastered at the same time I was having my hair firmly yanked up into a tortuous pompadour. I had a half-pint carton of milk in my lap, and when he squeezed behind me to get out, I pulled the flimsy director's chair up closer to the dresser to give him more room and spilled the milk on my lap. Luckily I was still wearing my own jeans. That was just the beginning. Later, outside, I met John Heard, who was to play my father, and Sissy

Spacek, who was cast as Carolyn Cassady. We all had plenty of time to gab in the sun, like children dressed up for Sunday School—metamorphosed into stiff anachronistic manikins. I helped John practice his Jack lip, showing him one of the few things I knew about my father, which was the way he stuck out his lower lip, easy for me because I had inherited it. And Sissy and I struck up a conversation, trading childhood stories: hers about Texas, in a husky drawl which I found to be hypnotic, and mine about New York. Meanwhile hoards of L.A. weirdos were pestering Sissy about her role as Carrie and asking her for autographs, and some energetic photographer was snapping rolls of photos of the two of us sitting on a packing crate.

Finally, we were allowed to enter the Acropolis Café. Yards of thick black cyclopsian equipment were dragged and wheeled into the cool, high-ceilinged place, where everyone again waited and waited—this time sitting at tables. Then the holy trinity took their places next to the biggest cyclops. The rest of us were supposed to comprise the background, blurred anonymous figures. My job was to sit at a table where two guys were playing a game of chess: to follow their moves like a cat, then to look mildly bored and giggle occasionally in my slinky beige crepe dress with pearl embroidery and massive shoulder pads, three-tone high heels, and heavily sprayed hairdo. We were all told to puff like mad on our Camel straights to produce a thick, smoke-filled atmosphere, and females were instructed to kiss a red blotch of lipstick onto the ends of their cigs.

Nick Nolte startled us all with a bout of spasmodic stamping and shuffling of feet, and drumming on the table, a curiously dynamic way of clearing his head—or, perhaps, essence of Neal Cassady popping through? Then he'd shout, "Okay, ready!" and the time machines would roll.

Either I was slowly asphyxiating from the Camel smoke, or toxic chemicals in the makeup were infiltrating my bloodstream, but gazing up at the lazily revolving black fans in the pressed waffle tin ceiling—I forgot *everything*. All I knew was, there I was, Camel burning in the ashtray, surrounded by outdated housewives in pincurlers and scarves, in some strangely contrived bubble of time when I wasn't even *born* yet. I experienced a disturbing notion: could I be my own mother? And who is that dark-haired man over there, pouting in baggy blue pants, talking about poetry to the blond couple? My father? My absentee husband? Where is this? California? Colorado? New York? What is this? Who am I?

"—I'm drunk, in the middle of the afternoon—" The husky golden Texas twang of the blond woman brought me reeling back to reality, the dubious reality of a movie set, spotlights softened with smoke spirals. . . . *Oh, that's right, I'm just an extra. Extra, extra, read all about it!*

That afternoon I wandered home up Hollywood Boulevard in milk-stiff pants, with spray-stiff hair, feeling like some kind of a doll that had been starched and pressed flat, two dimensional, and escaped from a toy-store window. But I also felt fulfilled in a funny way, as though the Neptunian illusions of Tinseltown had wrapped my father in Technicolor celluloid and brought him back to me, special delivery, straight into my arms.

23

October of '78 saw me packing up again . . . just as these star-studded hills were threatening to absorb me. Sixteen months was a long time for me to stay in any one place. Something in my shaky DNA usually compelled me to leave places sooner, in keeping with a childhood peppered with evictions and upheavals of all sorts. After the amnesia on the set of *Heartbeat*, I had begun to work as an extra all over L.A., calling a magic number every morning to find out where the films were being shot that day. Stars were fairly twinkling out of the woodwork that fall, inviting me to parties at art deco mansions that looked more like yachts—but something was missing. I had to see my mother.

On a bus again, going north this time, I suddenly remembered why I'd vowed never to go by bus *ever* again—but it was too late. In many crummy cafés, truck stops, and depots, I barely preserved my sanity by scribbling on napkins. Where was I going now? All at once my life appeared before me as a worthless string of pilgrimages here—there—anywhere. Was it true, what an old lover had said, that I was running away from something? But what was wrong with running *to* things? Sure, I was running—running to my mother. And what are mothers for if not to run to when a soul feels forsaken and misunderstood by the entire world?

The road whizzed endlessly by, molecule by molecule, tar blob after gravel speck after pebble after atom of yellow paint. I watched this dizzying procession from the greasy window and suddenly felt very alone. I thought of how a map of the world, this country in particular, would look if one were to draw red lines where I'd been. It would look like an airline flight pattern! You'd hardly be able to make out the towns. WHY? Could it really be my father's blood? How thoughtful of him to bequeath me this restless blood, never bothering to tell me how it works. He might at least have included an owner's manual! A rubber band tightened in my chest, eliciting tears from tired eyes. But I couldn't cry now—the weirdo across the aisle was watching, waiting for some sign of vulnerability to prey on.

An infinity of muggy stuffy seconds passed slowly, but once past they were as gone as gone could be. I stood on the faded red porch of 605½ North Ruby Street in Ellensburg, Washington, bags set down, admiring the light bulb and the snow shovel and the flimsy screen door with the awe-filled scrutiny of a time traveler. I pressed the rusty bell and listened with delight as it buzzed deep in the recesses of the house, arousing my unsuspecting mother.

"Who *is* it?" her eternally girlish voice rang out.

"Fullerbrushman!" I bellowed in my best Ralph Cramdenese. But that didn't fool her.

"David! Your sister's back!" I could hear her yelling excitedly as she descended the stairs.

"Which one?" came the gruff reply.

"Oh—the big one—I mean the little one. I mean your oldest

sister who is the littlest. . . ." My mother was all flustered and harebrained. I loved to see her that way.

"Is it really you?" she asked, unbarricading the door.

"Well, let's see. I think so, but you can't be too sure about these things." I hugged her, and felt her sharp shoulderbones padded by the red sweatshirt.

"Hey, you guys are really coming up in the world. Staircases and everything! Whatever happened to the shack out in Kittitas?"

"Oh, Jan, there's so much to tell you—this calls for a new pot of coffee. See? I still have the same blue pot you gave me. Now, you mustn't call it a shack, it was a house— Yes, *was*. The whole lot's been bulldozed. . . . Is your book done yet?"

"No, almost. But I was in a movie . . . and I met Sissy Spacek. Hey, David, I've got something for you."

"More foreign coins?"

"Guess again." I pulled a lavender plastic bag out of thin air— " 'Frederick's of Hollywood?!' " they read, aghast—and out of that came "A genuine fig leaf from Sycamore Avenue . . . complete with two fresh figs."

"Well, I've heard of crotchless panties, but this beats all!" said my mother as David blushed and held it up to himself.

"Well, I guess I'll go try them on. . . ."

It took all of three days to bring one another abreast of the events of the past three years, and then we got down to the business of Thanksgiving, compliments of the dumpster. One brisk November evening, David gleefully took me to see the treasure trove next door: a mammoth bin of supermarket rejects, consistently replenished with everything from foil-wrapped pots of live chrysanthemums to whole boxes of perfectly virgin Chiquita bananas to loads of half-pint cartons of whipping cream that weren't even past pull date! We got into the habit of climbing up the garbage-smeared rungs each night (this was the high point of the day). With inevitable stifled whoops of delight, we'd dive in and quickly gather our forbidden harvest in used boxes and crates, to scramble out, hands frozen, breath huffing in icy plumes, and hurry the mere half block back to Ruby Street with wondrous booty to dump at our mother's feet. The staircase was already lined with multicolored pots of chrysanthemums, one to each step. And on the night we came home with the cream a new pastime was born.

Neither David nor I had any idea what we should do with all the little cartons: how could we possibly stomach such a quantity of whipped cream before it went bad? But mother knew best—and with a fiendish glow in her eyes she declared, BUTTER. So for the next week, all we did, it seemed, was fill mason jars with cream and shake them manually. While talking or watching TV, even while soaking in the bathtub, each of us had to have a jar in hand. It was like a cause—we were the Butter Underground. Shaking the jarful of cream was kind of boring for a few minutes. But then, almost imperceptibly, a change would take place: the monotonous sloshing would stop, and you'd have a jar of whipped cream in your hands, all opaque and mysterious, of even weight. If you shook it really vigorously for a few more seconds, breaks would begin to appear in the cream, and then came a high-pitched sloshing. Before you knew it a big ball of pure butter was thudding back and forth in a pool of milk.

It was a rewarding process, and pretty soon we had amassed a freezerful of one-pound blocks of sweet butter, enough for all the holiday baking, plus the surprise byproduct of several gallons of lovely milk. All this time David had been wracking his brains to figure out an easier way to make our alchemical magic. One snowy afternoon he tied one of the jars inside a box, then tied the box to the ornate iron treadle of our mother's old Singer sewing machine and sat there, treadling away, churning butter with his foot. He couldn't resist the temptation to say, "Look, Ma, no hands!"

24

On New Year's Eve 1979 I went to a party at Melvin's house—yes, good old Melvin whom I hadn't seen since Bertrand and I left him in Dogtown when we went to Morocco. It seemed he had made amazing progress since then; namely, he had been adopted by a woman—a mother with three children with no daddy. Despite Melvin's atrocious habits and lack of personal hygiene, Carnelian fell madly in love with him. It was just the stroke of luck he needed after a sad childhood, the nuthouse, and a derelict adolescence.

Now Melvin was instant family man and lover-boy . . . just add *beer*. And the best part was, he still didn't have to work. Carnelian collected welfare—so, Melvin could listen to his ever-growing jazz collection in much the same way he used to, except that now there was a woman to cook for him and sleep with him, and a passel of leprechauns to entertain him and knock over his pedestal ashtray.

Bertrand was at the party too. I hadn't seen him for two years.

He appeared taller and more handsome than he had in Tacoma when I saw him last, in the hallway of my apartment on Pine Street. And he had a whole battery of new tales to tell. In New York that winter of '77 he had been working as a janitor in a whorehouse on Forty-second Street. Everyone at the party was transfixed as he related the story of how he had been ordered by the madame to repair some wiring in the wall and had to crawl through pitch darkness on his knees with pairs of rat's eyes watching him, cockroaches skittering over his hands. When all of a sudden the wall gave way and a trap door crashed open, he nearly fell out into the dark theater where X-rated movies were being shown. The small audience, startled, turned around to see what the commotion was, just in time for him to see—and for them to miss—a larger-than-life-sized cock, filling the whole screen, spurt like Vesuvius.

I watched Bertrand and his crescent of attentive admirers, noticing that his sense of drama had been honed to a fine edge since I'd met him. I was glad for all three of us—glad that we had split up and gone our separate ways for a while, instead of clinging together needlessly and crowding each other out like three basil seedlings in the same small pot.

There was someone else that night at Melvin's party who caught my eye. A quiet, intense young man was reading bedtime stories to Carnelian's daughter. He was Stan Robson, a dance student and piano player who had grown up in the Kittitas valley. He had already become fast friends with Bertrand, since they were doing janitorial work together at the Central Washington dorms. Now Bertrand came over and made some crass remarks about how Stan had better not mess around with his wife "or else, Goddamnit! . . ." which elicited fresh waves of mirth from the party organism.

On the way home that first steely below-zero morning of 1979, Stan and Bertrand and I skipped through the deserted frozen wasteland of the campus, past eerie pink lights on Eighth Avenue, laughing all the way. I felt at ease in a solid way next to Stan. He intrigued me, and the prospect of a new relationship was not at all unsavory . . . not any more so than the prospect of a new day—or even a New Year.

Jan, 1957

Jan, Albuquerque, 1994. *Photo by Jack Newsom.*

From left: Dave, Lillian, Joan and Jan, Violet. At Patsy and Dan Moony's House, Carmel, N.Y., 1957 ?

Hollywood, CA, 1978 ?

Chicago, June 1979. (*copyright © 1998 Gerald Nicosia*)

San Francisco, 1979. *(copyright © 1998 Gerald Nicosia)*

Greece, 1986 ?

Albuquerque

25

On a black and billowy February night I ran into Stan by the Liberty
Theater, the only cinema in Ellensburg. He was wearing a navy
blue captain's cap which accentuated his cobalt eyes fabulously in
the dim glow of the marquee. . . .

"Hi. Want to come up for tea and a bubble bath?" Stan asked,
with such an innocent air that I knew he'd never made such a
proposition to anyone else before in his life.

"Bubble bath, hmmm . . . ?" I raised my eyebrows and looked
him up and down. He was a dead ringer for Le Petit Prince, with
that scarf around his neck blowing in the wind, stars in his blue
eyes. . . .

I tucked my arm in his, and we floated up the stairs to his
apartment over the movie house—strangely like a New York tenement here in the middle of this farming valley.

Ahhh . . . if only we humans could know when to stop. Back

then on that enchanted evening with the candlelight, the gleaming eyes, and the novelty of a new love . . . a new tea . . . a new tub . . . surprise of smooth bubbles and the uncanny innocence of a man who seemed more like a sorcerer's apprentice than a man— how could we have imagined what was to come? Neither of us could possibly have foreseen the move, the bird, the loofah plant . . . the arguments and tears, spliced with brief fragments of ease. The hatred of each other's differences—my fear of his psychotic breaks—senseless abuse of proximity, ultimately breeding contempt. The fire. The jealousy. The end.

But on that night when all was still so young, so pure, like a virgin patch of snow, as I devilishly seduced this angel through his impeccable shorts, how could I have suspected that the very naiveté that so fascinated me was to become the trait I would end up so passionately despising? The manic neatness of Stan, reflected in everything he did, at first viewed as refreshingly atypical for a man, was to eventually drive me batty. It was the night of a solar eclipse, February 26, 1979, when I took Stan Robson's twenty-four-year-old cherry to the strains of Holst's *Saturn*. A karmic accident—conducted by Fate? Or Sir Adrian Bolt?

In April we moved into a house that we fondly referred to as "Old Gray." There we had lovely south-facing bay windows where sun streamed in on Stan's parakeet, a big backyard, an old-fashioned porch that wrapped around the front and side of the house. It was an ideal setup for us less-than-ideal inhabitants—and now, at least we had a nice big stage on which to act out all our dramas. We shared a love of thunderstorms, it turned out, and that summer of '79 there were plenty of them to provide backdrops for us. Stan always put on Mussorgsky full blast and we'd sit out on the porch sipping Aquavit. Then the arguments would begin. I would usually wind up running barefoot three blocks through the crashing thunder to my mother's house on Ruby, convinced that Stan was mad.

One day he found my manuscript and began reading the parts

about Miguel threatening to kill me in South America—he was in a jealous rage that I was writing about a previous boyfriend. At first, I laughed in disbelief—told him to get serious. But when I noticed the twisted glare in his eyes and the cold sweat on his upper lip, I took him at face value—he *was* serious! This behavior of Stan's was contagious, and I found myself doing dramatic things, like taking the whole 250 pages of manuscript out onto the front sidewalk and setting it on fire, just to make him feel better. (Of course I had a copy at my mother's.) And so it was that we moved out of Old Gray after only a few bittersweet months—the bird had flown away and summer was over. The tragedy was that we both loved the house, but not each other.

Yet we stayed together for some unknown reason. By the time we were moving into our third apartment, Stan had already decided that I was an unreliable flake like his father, and I had noticed that he washed dishes exactly like his mother, with the same proper butt and martyrlike expression. And I was already developing a raving crush on his brother Lawrence (hadn't this happened somewhere before?), who was Stan's perfect opposite: capable, masculine, gruff, down-to-earth, whereas Stan was sensitive, complex, talented, mentally unstable, and feminine. And *prissy*. Why is that such an awful trait in a man? Stan was most definitely prissy. I watched him wash the dishes, standing at the sink with that pole-up-the-ass posture, his dancer's butt clenched ever so tight (or was it just naturally shaped that way?), his mouth pursed, his whole prissy being singularly addressed to the task of *washing dishes*.

It occurs to me that Stan reminds me of my grandmother . . . For a few moments I am back in Wappingers Falls, New York, in 1956 in my grandmother's pristine kitchen, riding my tricycle over the shiny linoleum floor of black-and-white checkerboard squares. Then I see Granny's derriere. She's standing at the sink washing dishes in a gray wool skirt, and it's shaking. Shaking from the vigorous motions of washing dishes, just like it shakes when she brushes her teeth at night after the *Perry Como Show.*

My head is at ass level, and I can't resist. I climb off my three-wheeled chariot and approach stealthily, glass of water in hand. Then, ever so carefully, I hold up the glass to her quivering buttocks draped properly in gray wool and tip it a tad until a quarter-sized wet spot appears.

"Janet!" Granny spins around. I've wrecked her composure. "Why did you do that?!" Little Janet shrugs. She really doesn't know why, because there was not thought involved, only pure impulse—the impulse to anoint those quaking hemispheres, those tangible manifestations of her Protestant work ethic. . . .

So I watch Stan wash the dishes, and wonder how he would react to such an anointment. I am quite sure that his composure would be wrecked as well. But I am older now—and Janet should know better! I can't stand it anymore.

"Hey, I'll do the rest of those dishes," I offer.

"Oh, that's all right, they're almost done anyway." Stan sighs and I notice he has sweat on his upper lip. Probably clammy palms, too, only they're deep in hot sudsy water now. Stan is afraid I'll break something. I've broken so many wine glasses in the past year. He makes me nervous.

Later at his parents' house, he plays the piano—Ravel, Debussy, Chopin, Rachmaninoff—marvelously. Amazingly complicated structures of notes issue from those sweaty fingers, feverish brain, balding head, cobalt eyes. Now the thin sandy wisps of hair are damp on Stan's high forehead. All of his psychosis is pardonable when he plays the piano. A few notes go awry during "Le Tombeau de Couperin." He curses bitterly and stops. The people in the sun-filled room implore him to go on, me included.

"Oh, I'm out of practice!" he complains.

"Oh no—it's beautiful—how can you say that?" But I know that in Stan's mind he is performing solo, on stage, before an audience of discerning musicians—and a few notes *do* matter.

An ungodly rumbling is heard in the driveway, and a huge black truck appears in the window, lurches to a halt. A strong, scruffy young man bounds into the house, infecting everyone with inexplicable joy.

"Larry! Larry's home!"

"Hey Stanley! How's it goin', man?" The frail pianist is swept up off his bench, and the two brothers embrace like mother and father.

A man is walking through the pastures with a steady, capable gait. He walks as though he himself invented the land beneath his feet. He's on his way to the shed, to do something unquestionably important, be it clearing out boards, feeding the goats, welding a trough. . . . Whatever Larry does, he seems to do it with sheer earthbound ease. I wonder fleetingly as I watch him through the window, Would he seem so quintessentially masculine if I could have him? Half the attraction could very well be his indifference to me as a woman.

Off he goes, taking his well-formed independent self to some invisible realm of practicality which he must enjoy, alone. This apparent ability of his, to do things all by himself with no need for feedback from others, has won my respect and admiration to such an extent that I don't even seek out his company. I dare not bother Larry with what I imagine he would think trivial. I steer clear, giving him space, creating my own distance, shooting him a furtive look now and again, a short friendly remark or smile. Hoping inwardly that we might find ourselves flung together by happy accident someday—snowed into a cabin under an avalanche and having to sleep in the same bed out of dire necessity—and then, perhaps I could show him . . . how . . . what . . . How what?

My daydreaming had brought me up short. My projections on

Larry had canceled themselves out, like an algebraic equation. Nothing could ever happen between Larry and me because we were both so stubborn by nature that no one would ever make a first move: neither of us would want to risk vulnerability.

So. It would just have to remain an impossible daydream. I continued to watch him, reaching out with invisible hands to ruffle the thick head of straw blond hair, never combed, always slightly dusty with work; solid forearms encased in plaid flannel shirtsleeves; sturdy bowed legs in stovepipe jeans, muddy combat boots; rough hands. . . . For all I knew, he could have been thinking the same thing about me.

Sunday morning. Stan and I were sitting down to a lazy breakfast of French toast in our apartment overlooking the church. It looked like we were in for another thunderstorm. But by this time we had long since ceased to let thunderstorms affect us the way we had in Old Gray. Huge billowing mountains of clouds were massing in the south, creating an ominous backdrop for the church steeple and all the people in their brightly colored Sunday best. Lightning zipped through the heavy gray curtain that seemed to be lowering over their heads as the church sucked the last of them in like a vacuum cleaner swallows bits of confetti.

Stan ran around the house opening all the windows. "Ah, this is going to be a good one—I can tell!" He actually rubbed his hands together in anticipation.

An hour later, I looked up from my typewriter and he from his Schoenberg. Still no rain. But the streetlamps had automatically switched on—at 11 AM! This was no ordinary storm. The intense darkness reminded me of rainy schooldays in Manhattan, when for some reason we all wound up shoeless in the gymnasium in yellow electric light.

"Wait a minute. Is there an eclipse today?" I said, and Stan looked in the almanac. No eclipse. And instead of ozone, a funny sulfuric smell was seeping in through the window screens. We ran to the north window like trapped birds and saw the thin strip of light that remained on the horizon. . . . Our eyes grew wide with apprehension. Could this be IT? The END?

We flipped on the TV: the Tuttle River, full of trees and mud, crashing, roiling; a frantic announcer babbling that a cataclysm had happened hours earlier, hundreds of miles to the southeast of us—Mount Saint Helens. It was May 18, 1980.

"I repeat—do not go outside unless it is absolutely necessary!" the announcer warned. We were being blanketed by the ash. We methodically closed all the windows, with strange identical looks of awe on our faces, and quietly proceeded to don bandanas bandit style and venture out—almost as if in defiance of the warning—padding through the deathly gray snowfall. It was amazing how a tiny movement would set off a plume of ash into the air, rather like more explosions in miniature. The stuff was so fine and yet so heavy: if you touched a car's windshield, covered with an inch-thick layer, the whole sheet of ash would instantly collapse, sending up blinding puffs of it. It wasn't every day a human could experience this firsthand . . . and neither of us had respiratory ailments.

Stan wanted to check on his grandmother, who was senile. And sure enough, as we neared her house, there she was out on the front porch with nothing over her face, sweeping the front porch. "My lands—have you ever seen such dirty snow?" she said as Stan coaxed her back inside and tried to drum into her head what happened. But she just giggled and kept repeating, "My lands, it snowed!"

So we walked all the way out to his parents' house, through a ghostly landscape of ashen pastures, and surveyed the garden: strawberry plants all buried in ash and lilacs bowing from the weight of it. We shook it off and scanned the gray valley. Would it ever be the same? What about the pond we always went to swim in? What kind of a summer would this be?

In a few days the wind started blowing, making it really dangerous to go out. You could get literally sandblasted. It was a first-class mess. Everyone wore bandanas in the supermarkets, even in the banks. I was amazed that no one thought of holding a stick-up. It would have been the perfect opportunity, with fifty other masked bandits standing in line.

Just as we all became convinced that the valley was permanently ruined and we would have to move away, it *rained*. And all that remained of the volcano were little residual strips of ash in the gutters. How could we have forgotten the curative powers of rain? In fact, the Washington State wines of 1981 vintage would turn out to be quite special due to the high silica content of the ash that washed down into the soil.

Stan's brother Larry was using the ash for glazes on his pottery, which turned out a rosy glossy pink. I nearly broke my back lugging a small cardboard box of it upstairs as a present for him. (One cubic foot of it probably weighed close to fifty pounds.)

My mother and David had missed all of this madness—left for Oregon shortly before it happened. They had gone directly toward the volcano—and then a lot of it landed on us. Sometimes I wondered if they were responsible for the whole thing.

26

Stan and I had been together two years. In February of 1981 we moved into our fourth apartment, a sort of refurbished servants' quarters in back of one of the oldest houses in Ellensburg. Stan was making great strides as the soup chef at McCullough's French restaurant, and every day he seemed to invent a brand-new soup. His latest was banana, served hot with a touch of freshly grated nutmeg.

One quiet dawn we lay sleeping, deep in unknown bed reveries and dead to the world, when an unearthly noise shook us from sleep. A howling, screeching, high whine like ten banshees on the warpath seemed to surround us. We both leapt in mortal terror, stark naked, and stood in the middle of the bedroom frantically shouting "What?!" at each other and turning in bewildered circles.

Well, the whateveritwas died down, and we figured it was some horrendous thing that had happened next door. Stan got back into bed and I groggily went into the bathroom to pee. Still half asleep, though a bit shaken, I flushed the toilet, intending to return to bed—and, lo and behold—the godawful noise returned, even louder, accompanied this time by STEAM hissing madly out of the *toilet!* The nameless terror was so rare, so nightmarish—hardly ever are we confronted with phenomena that have *no* explanation—that I literally ejected from the bathroom, just in time to hear a loud POP. The porcelain toilet bowl had actually cracked, and boiling hot water was flooding onto the floor.

Well, needless to say, this called for a plumber. As it turned out, the culprit was not poltergeists but the ancient water heater in the main house, a very large gas-heated monster which somehow had gotten stuck ON and superheated all the water in all the pipes of both houses, melting the little plastic gadgets in the newer toilet tanks and filling them too. The noise that woke us up had been the neighbor making the mistake of flushing his toilet. We had been privy to a real old-fashioned plumbing disaster à la Laurel and Hardy.

And so it was that from the place where the toilet had blown up only a week before, I set off one fine morning to do my time at the county jail. With the book finished, I finally had enough money to hire a good lawyer to clear up the felony that had been hanging over my head like a cloud of doom for two years. And it was a good thing I hadn't just turned myself in cold—the lawyer got my sentence reduced from five *years* to five *days*. I could do these five days right here in good old Ellensburg. No need for nightmarish Tacoma lockups.

I kissed Stan good-bye, and he went off to work, at once proud of me for facing the law I'd broken and disapproving of this girlfriend of his who went off in the morning to jail instead of to ballet class. I marched through the stark lawful awfulness of corridors, and they wasted no time in whisking me right into Cell One. A huge empty cell all to myself. At first I felt like a child left in a playpen and busied myself with drawings and daydreams. But the novelty soon wore off. Then dinnertime rolled around, and I knew what a grind

I was in for. I had expected the food to be bad, but never imagined it could be *this* bad: wretched tomato macaroni slop like they used to have in the public schools of Manhattan; no vegetable, green or otherwise; a heap of false generosity in the form of white mattress-stuffing bread; and, last and definitely least—the worst coffee in the universe. Warm brown water in a scratched yellow plastic cup.

Maybe sleep would make the time go faster, I thought, hiding from the fluorescent lights under a scratchy wool blanket on the unyielding striped pad of the upper bunk. Later, unable to sleep, I rigged up an ingenious shield for the toilet, which was completely exposed to anyone walking by: the blanket and shower curtain strung to the bunk with rubber bands—deep down imitating my mother's behavior in the TB hospital in Oneonta, New York. The story she had told me many years ago when I was a toddler had stuck with me all these years: of how she had wrapped strips of bacon around her electric coffee pot, despite condescending glares from the psychiatrist. She was proud of her contraption, which reheated the bacon while the coffee was brewing, and that was all that mattered.

Next was the light. In pencil I sketched an Egyptian eye on a piece of white paper and stuck it in the glaring square fixture above the toilet—romantic mood lighting for my suite. By now, hunger was wreaking havoc in my solar plexus, and the only consolation was that if I had opted to eat that dreadful slop earlier, something far worse than hunger might be wreaking havoc in its stead. As I drifted off to sleep, I wondered dimly what sort of Godforsaken crud they'd serve for breakfast. . . .

Just as I had finally succeeded in entering a blissful dimension of boardwalks and ferris wheels half submerged in surf, where people ate lavender cotton candy . . .

COCKSUCKERS!! A horribly enraged bellowing jarred me back to gray celldom. It took a few moments for the shock to register as anger. Meanwhile, the being in the next cell was kicking up quite a ruckus.

"Sonofabitchin' mothjerfuckers I'll kill yuhs! Goddamnit!" Loud banging on something metal followed. This must have gone one for ten minutes with no letup, during which time the other prisoners became rather perturbed.

"Hey! Why dontchoo shut the fuck up, man, an' let us sleep!"

"Yeah, cut the noise—shithead!"

But that only made him madder. His constant banging and wailing was like an air raid siren on the brain.

"LISTEN, ASSHOLE!" My female voice sliced through the base rumbles and echoing growls like a laser . . . and for three seconds there was blessed silence.

Then, "Hoos dis bitch? Ain't no bitch gonna tell me—"

I crept up right to the edge where my cell met his and threw a plastic saucer between his bars. It clattered nicely. I could hear guys way down at the other end murmuring to each other, "Hey man, there's a *woman* in here."

"Goddamnit!" roared the drunken newcomer with a hurt-sounding yodel in his voice. "Can't a guy get no peace nowhere?" He trailed off into an unintelligible slur, and everyone forgot about him for a while.

"Hey, sweetie, what cell you in?"

"Cell One," I answered automatically—realizing it was a mistake before it was even out of my mouth.

Instantly about eight different male voices were calling "Hey Cell One!" in motley unison.

Now the guy in Cell Two woke up again . . .

"Gaad. Damn. Sonoffa. Blishh. . . . Lemmee outta here! Aaaaaggghhrrll!" More banging.

"Aw, come on, you can do better than that!"

"Whatsamatta, ya tired already?" Somebody had a brilliant idea, and all the others quickly joined in with the reverse psychology tack.

"Yeah, King Kong, let's have some more drums. . . . Louder!"

Cell Two finally passed out in earnest, and once again I crawled back into dreamland, institutional toilet paper wadded up in my ears, to the lullaby of far-off voices:

"Hey, Cell One. What's your name, honey?"

I decided to take advantage of the freedom to break my "commitment" into two parcels, and a day later I came merrily home to Stan, for a night in the real world and some decent food. The cracked toilet had been replaced by a brand spanking new one . . . and Stan told me about his latest creation at the restaurant—papaya lime consommé. For the second stretch, I smuggled in some carrot and celery sticks, since they never searched me because I was on a commitment. But this also meant that they were in no hurry to put me in, and I wound up having to wait over an hour to be rebooked—during which time the carrots and celery strapped to my legs were cutting off circulation. By the time I got back into my cell, the precious raw vegetables were all limp and wilted and I had deep red marks on my shins.

I laughed and said out loud to myself, "Well, that'll teach you to go around writing bad checks!"

After I got out of jail, I wandered around Ellensburg alone a good deal feeling forlorn and not knowing why . . . and then one day as I passed the stately old red Victorian on Ruby Street it hit me—with my mother gone, this town just wasn't the same. Her eccentric spirit had relocated, from the Kittitas valley to the Willamette valley, and now my spirit would follow hers once again.

In April of '81 Stan borrowed his brother Larry's motorcycle, a Honda 350, and we went on a rollicking relentless trip to Eugene, Oregon, along the back roads of Yakima and Granger, down through the Columbia River gorge, past signs that seemed to say as we whizzed past in the rain CAUTION—SEVERAL WILD GHOSTS when in fact what they really said was CAUTION—SEVERE WIND GUSTS.

27

The Bethel Triangle neighborhood on Saturday was quiet, its streets shining and deeply engrossed in the business of drizzle. My feet pattered unnoticed through puddles that dimly reflected the underside of a white umbrella. Toward the tracks beneath tall petulant trees, through the drenched backyards of Eugene, Oregon, I wandered like a wet shadow on my way to work.

Squeals and screeches from brakes of freight cars taunted my ears, muffled slightly by the mist as I trudged, half asleep, in the same black galoshes I'd worn in the Washington corn cannery seven years before. Now they glistened like sea lions with each step. Suddenly I decided to go through the switching yards, responding to a childish taste for the forbidden, for paths seldom taken—but above all, for blackberries.

Hidden birds peeped from sodden bushes, punctuating the metallic sounds of Trainsong Park like Morse code. I arrived at the soaked and slippery plank that served as a footbridge across the ditch . . . peering down in quick horror of anticipation to glimpse what fresh atrocity floated therein. Today it was Kentucky fried chicken, the same plastic baby doll of last week with green mold forming in its eye sockets, and a dead possum, bloated and losing its hair. The family who lived in the prefab housing next to the ditch were forever tossing things into the water, and it was fast becoming an open sewer. I felt no qualms about referring to them as white trash.

Shuddering with revulsion, I nearly lost my balance on the narrow plank and turned my attention instead to the bright beacon beaming up the track. Train coming—quick decision called for—to wait, or not to wait. It looked like a long one, fifty or more cars strung together. Without another thought I sprinted across the track, alarming the engineer.

BWAAAAAAAAAAAAAAAAAAHHHHHHHHHHHHHH!

I crashed like a jackrabbit into the blackberry brambles on the other side. Catching my breath in the rainy thicket, I savored the heavy clunking vibrations of the train—mammoth iron and steel wheels in a dense grind of rhythmic interplay. It beat messages through earth and gravel, reaching up into my footsouls as I stood there, riveted to the metal-on-stone serenade.

For some time I dawdled along that strip of railroad brush, mesmerized by gleaming purple clusters nestled in the leaves. I felt like a bear braving bees to find honey, ripping my hands on thorns, rummaging obsessed through the perilous bramblery. At the end of the track I scrambled up onto Roosevelt Avenue like a wild woman, fingers and lips dyed violet.

It was good not to have Stan's severe presence hovering about, making me feel guilty at every turn. Even this, what I was doing now, he would disapprove of. I knew I had made the right move in coming down here to live with my mother and brother. There were no wine glasses to break on Bell Avenue, and even if there were it wouldn't matter. There'd be no tight-lipped sighs or shaking of heads (except maybe in jest). Mommy and David would just laugh, shrug, and the broken glass would be swept up—probably not even put into the garbage right away. It might well sit in a dusty corner under the broom for days in my mother's house.

And I knew why, too: Granny, my mother's mother, had been just like Stan. She disapproved of everything little Joanie ever did, every move she made—and marrying my father was no exception. A beatnik! Heavens to Betsy! My mother was still rebelling at this in many ways: by painting the bathroom ultramarine just for the hell of it with old dried-up chunks of paint, smashing the color onto the walls as though with giant crayons—burying the smoke detector in the compost heap—using an ice pick to open the refrigerator—demolishing the living room couch—planting a jungle of tomato plants in the driveway. Really I should thank Granny for such an eccentric mother.

Careening past lumberyards in a lurching green rhombus packed with nurse's aides bound for Sacred Heart Hospital . . . several nodding dreams later it was my stop: The Excelsior Café. This was one of the two jobs I could remember actually being *glad* to go to; the other was at the racetrack, where I groomed horses in '73. Around back I went, past the garbage with its ever-so-familiar smell, pavement stained with black grease, dozens of bottles holding the dregs of rare vintage wines, mounds of spent gourmet coffee grounds. All these ingredients contributed to a unique mix of odors which welcomed me—saying, Yes, this is the right place . . . come on in . . .

Clattering down worn stairs into the basement, out of the chill drizzle and into the warm, secure ovenish interior of the bakery, was edifying. All alone, so early. Having a clean apron tied snugly around my waist was a sensation harkening back to wearing dry diapers. Time to make a brand-new Chemex pot of mocha Harrar and heat up one of yesterday's croissants. Then into the walk-in to hoist plastic five-gallon buckets of fermenting French bread dough, and I'd grab the heavy old scale, CLUNK it down on the formidable butcher block bread board (which was long enough to accommodate a whole Frankenstein monster), and, first allowing myself to disdainfully flick some of the janitor's cigarette ashes off *my* board, I was ready to begin.

One by one, I chopped eighty-seven chunks of dough, each weighing a pound, rolled them into little torpedo shapes, lined them up on the floured board, while taking intermittent gulps of strong coffee, talking to myself, listening to the radio. This was my morning regimen and I loved it. Later, when I had rolled the torpedoes into two-foot-long serpents, popped all the air bubbles out, and laid them side by side in the proof box to rise, there were some hazards to reckon with. One of these was the convection oven, which held four huge trays at once. In three months I had burned myself three times, and my arms were already beginning to bear the marks of the trade. If I worked here a year, would I have twelve brands from the baker's iron? After brushing the fat white serpents with yellow eggwash I slashed them diagonally thrice, and when they were forging in the furnace there was always more dough to be made. This was possible only with Hobart.

Hobart was a monstrous aluminum being, crouched permanently in one corner, four feet tall, and holding in his strong gray arms a barrel-sized bowl. Sticking down into this was, among other attachments, his twisted proboscis of a dough hook. Hobart was a dangerous though well-meaning character. Once the sixty pounds of dough was getting the daylights beaten out of it, hopefully you knew not to reach in for any reason—not even for a tiny second, to pinch a tiny crumb. Because if that hook of his ever caught hold of a finger, or an apron string, or God forbid an arm—well, let's just say that the horror stories were enough to keep *me* at a respectful distance. And hopefully you also remembered to check the speed.

Two was right for dough. But one day the guy who came to make sausage had left it on four and when I flipped it on, full of a fifty-pound bag of flour and one-and-a-half gallons of water, half a cup of yeast and a quarter cup of salt

FWABOOOOOOOOOOOOOPPPPHHH!

the whole basement was a blizzard of flour, blinding white billows everywhere. I had held my breath for fear of contracting white lung, a bona fide disease that bakers get, just like coal miners get black lung.

Add to all these hazards the omnipresent blue haze of burning cornmeal from the bottoms of the pans (a fragrance I loved, associated as it was with feelings of accomplishment), and there were hazards aplenty.

All in all though, it was truly rewarding when at 11 AM I proudly bore trays of oven-fresh aromatic loaves upstairs to a kitchenful of appreciative cooks and waiters, their days just beginning and mine all but over.

It was at that particular bread-bearing moment on July 20, 1982, as I trudged kitchenward with a load of golden brown egg-shellacked baguettes, when the dishwasher met me halfway, his eyes wide as saucers, and said breathlessly, "Ken Kesey is here, and he says he wants to see you!"

Waiters were craning their necks from the soup wells and the whole restaurant was abuzz. I dumped off the bread and met him in the hallway for the first time. Big and bearlike with a red T-shirt on, he seemed to fill the cramped corridor. We both felt stifled in there and decided to talk outside. Once we were out in the bright sunny parking lot, he extended a muscular hand, and with a momentary hesitation I offered mine, realizing that it was still encrusted with flour and dried dough. But Ken made a point of grabbing it anyway, with a laugh and the hearty roughness of one who lives on a farm and runs a yogurt factory.

"I spoke to your mother this morning and she told me where to find you," he growled benevolently.

"Well, this is the place, all right," I said, nodding toward the wine-redolent garbage can, feeling as though I already knew him very well.

"I hear you're going to the writers' conference in Boulder."

"Hmmm . . . I've had a few invitations," I said, picturing those envelopes with the embossed red Tibetan wheel.

"I thought maybe we could go together," he offered. We leaned against a red convertible in the parking lot, pensive for some moments. . . . The prospect of going to Boulder was beginning to sound more attractive to me. After all, it wasn't every day that I ran into someone who actually had known my father, remembered him in the flesh. Imagined visions of the famous magic bus flitted through my mind. Perhaps Kesey and I could cook up some comparable shenanigans—and take up where my father had left off?

"Well . . . if you're going . . ."

Ken's enthusiasm rubbed off on me, and for the next few minutes we stood there squinting in the sun, he in muddy boots and me in flour-dusted apron, chatting like old pals and making these sudden Colorado plans. When he left I felt reinvigorated, like a mechanical doll whose key has been rewound . . . set to walk in a new direction.

28

I spent that last sultry week in Trainsong Park before going to Boulder playing with my little brother, who wasn't so little anymore. David was a full six inches taller than I, in fact—and now that he was life-sized, he was more fun to play with. There was no dumpster nearby to raid like there had been in Ellensburg, but we found plenty to do. We sat around for hours making weird noises through a giant cardboard tube and then recorded them; we put the TV set upside down in a box with magnifying glasses and succeeded in projecting a hugely perfect movie on his bedroom door, through which our mother walked, and we bewildered her by yelling as she entered, coffee cup in hand, "Hey, you're in the way, we can't see the movie!"

We picked blackberries and made milk shakes in the blender, built deformed sculptures from old bicycle parts and hung them from the trees, took pictures of each other dressed in outlandish costumes. One day we just dug an enormous hole for no reason at all. Friends of our mother would come over and say, "You know, Joan, you're so lucky to have children of the same age." What they didn't know was that he was seventeen and I was thirty. Other neighbors saw us digging all day and asked us what we were doing.

"We digged dis ho!" David answered in his best Buckwheat imitation. "I be diggin' de ho wid de duht an' de shoveh aw day lawn!"

When the hole was done, six feet deep and five feet wide, we sat on the edge, listening to the squealing of brakes in the switching yards while our mother weeded peacefully under the filbert tree and her wash dried on the line. We didn't know what else to do with the hole, so we put the hose in it and filled it up with water. It seemed like a worthwhile thing to do, but all it accomplished was to provide a murky swimming pool for the worms and one more obstacle course for the backyard.

Shortly before I left for the conference in Colorado, I went to a Saturday market with David and made a big mistake: I was very hungry and I bought a grass brownie and ate the whole thing. While wolfing it down I was vaguely aware of all the little green specks in it, never imagining what the seemingly innocuous goody was going to do to me.

On the way home it hit. Like ten hits of acid. Like a ton of TNT. All at once my body just wasn't there. I could see it, but hard as I slapped and poked myself in the arm, face, leg, anywhere (creating quite a spectacle) there was *nothing*. Absolutely no sensation. I tried pinching myself till it should have hurt. Still nothing. Neither on the surface nor deep down. It was as if I had been dunked in a vat of novocaine and thoroughly soaked. But that was not all.

As I whispered to David, "I can't feel myself at *all!*" the bus driver was melting into his stool and people's heads were getting very small. The windows were plastered with blue intermeshing writhing hands and bat wings, and the whole world wobbled dangerously. The bus was making it worse. As we got off the bus, passengers gawked. I kept shaking my head vigorously, for fear that I might lose touch and disappear through a hole in the universe. I was hanging onto life by a tiny thread. Never in all my drug years had I experienced anything like that brownie! And worst of all, it was firmly lodged in my digestive system, being ever-so-slowly processed—an ingenious torture. All I could do was wait . . . for at least thirteen hours. Paranoia, aphasia, hallucinations—the trip had all the earmarks of a tetrahydrocannabinol overdose.

If I remained in public I was liable to get carted away to a nuthouse, so David took me home and put me to bed—definitely the wisest choice. In the big house right next door to my mother and brother, which I had rented for the month, I thrashed and floundered in my tiny bed, adrift in the black space of nonentityhood for an abbreviated eternitude of never. My mother and David checked in on me often, though I was in no condition to notice—much less distinguish a human being from my wood stove.

Many hours later (by normal reckoning), when I could almost talk but the words were still hopelessly scrambled and I might as well have been one of the first newts to crawl up on land—who should suddenly appear but *Stan*.

Evidently he had already gone to my mother's house expecting to find me there, and they had warned him of my highly unusual condition. He had insisted on visiting me anyway.

I was like someone possessed or having delirium tremens. . . . "What—oh . . . who? help! Oh I'm—no . . . you don't know—" I was dimly aware of how I must sound to him, but hopelessly unable to piece things together.

Stan was aghast—I didn't even remember his name! By morning most of the THC had evaporated from my poor wasted spirit, and I felt slightly precariously normal again. Stan had left in a huff, they said. Instead of feeling disappointed, I thought it was funny, hilarious even, that he had reacted this way—that such a disastrous coincidence had happened—that of all nights he should pick that one to come down unannounced from Washington. Talk about bad timing!

29

My first glimpse of the Flatirons in Boulder was under curling wisps of gray. There was an Indian curse: whoever lays eyes upon these sloping planes of rock for the first time when they're cloud-cloaked is doomed to return to them forever and ever. I stared into this beautiful doom and wondered how and when this place could ever feel like a curse to me. Could this be *home?*

I already knew that Eugene was definitely not my home, no matter how much my mother wanted me to stay or how much I loved playing with David. I had to find my own home now. The Kittitas valley in Washington State wasn't home anymore, nor was California, New Mexico, or New York. But this place, so dramatic, was doing something to me now . . . seducing me before I even unpacked my bags.

Funny—I'd had absolutely no preconception of Boulder, of how it would look or anything. All I knew was that it was where my *Gourmet* magazines came from.

Maybe I would never find a home again. Maybe Home was something intrinsically belonging to the past, never to be encountered again—something as lost as Father, as outdated as Husband.

The cab dropped me off. I knew that the address was 813 Maple, but preferred to toy with the idea that I was meandering aimlessly up and down the cool leafy streets of these Rocky Mountain foothills. Let's see . . . which one? I picked at imaginary random—and here in all the world . . . of all the Victorian front porches in Colorado, this one held a note for *me*. Magic.

Jan—
> Make yourself at home. I'll be back at 6:30.
>
> —Judy

I let go of the game now. It had run its course. The screen door beckoned to a dark wood-smelling foyer complete with ornately carved newel posts and creaky floorboards. I breathed deeply and stretched my back, totally unaware of the disheveled being watching from the couch, blending in with the cushions. Hardly breathing, his beady eyes peered through a tangled mass of white hair. The creature was playing his own little game that afternoon. An inner cue told him that now was the time to pounce—

In a white blur the Lhasa apso greeted me. I tried to calm him down, but that was like trying to stuff a jack-in-the-box back into its box the moment it pops. This Tibetan canine mascot of 813 Maple returned my greeting with a long pink scratch on the neck from one of his dull excitable claws, a fitting baptism for my arrival in Boulder.

Just as I was recovering from the dog's greeting and was treading gingerly into the living room, feeling something akin to nostalgia for the present, another being materialized—this one, however, was human: a short, sandy-haired young man wearing a pumpkin-colored jacket sped through the cool space of the foyer.

"Hi, I'm Malcolm, nice to meet you. I'm late for dinner with my girlfriend. See ya later!"

I've often wondered if it was that first impression—of a man whirling past me so fast that I couldn't quite see him, like a shooting star or a meteorite—that would make me into a huntress of sorts later . . . much later . . . far in the impossible future. A huntress who ultimately wants to slay her prey, perhaps because of this illusion, this blurring—and this man's subconscious desire to be chased. To be wanted: dead or alive.

At the grand reception at the Boulderado Hotel, after I had gotten quite mellow on Cuba libres in the six thousand feet of altitude which made me feel empty like a Christmas-tree ball . . . it was after I had wildly fallen into the white-suited lap of John Steinbeck, Jr., and cameras had flashed like deranged lightning bugs and Nanda Pivano had invited me to Italy, and scores of beat luminaries had twinkled their introductions and gone into eccentric orbits around my accidental halo, while in fact all I was doing was admiring the fabulous stained-glass ceiling of the Boulderado and dizzily trying to imagine how on earth they had built it. It was when the party was still in full swing but I'd had enough and wandered out into the unknown novelty of mountain summer night alone, glad to be leaving alone and unnoticed and aligning my radar for the walk down newly discovered foothill sidewalks. . . .

It was after all that. Someone was calling to me. I turned around and saw that it was Malcolm, now in a white jacket, but still sporting the same stark wintergreen smile.

"Wait! I'll walk you home."

Under the towering lush trees and over buckling slabs of pink granite we walked and talked. He told me that he was originally from Eugene. . . . Things seemed to be clicking together with amazing synchronicity, like a lucky win at the racetrack. In the deserted night kitchen with warm breezes coming through the back door, we had an innocuous tête-à-tête over herb tea. He was boyish, yet experienced. I was adventurous, yet idle. He noticed when I rolled my neck.

"Want a massage?"

"Oh, sure—I'd love one."

And up the stairs we went. The single bed had been made up with burgundy satin sheets for my arrival. In candlelight they were very inviting.

I lay face down under Malcolm's rough muscular hands, reveling in the massage and feeling a tremendous urge to *turn over*. I resisted this urge for twenty minutes, and when I eventually gave in, he was waiting for me. We slid right together like sea otters, amazing ourselves with the novelty of ourselves mirrored in sudden intimacy. Malcolm's slick, smooth operating seemed at first to be some superconscious refinement of lust. Could it be—possibly—*tantra?* He was a well-hung Buddhist plumber, so perhaps that wasn't so farfetched.

For the next four days of the conference, Malcolm appointed himself my escort, chauffeur, bodyguard, and lover. What I didn't know was that he had been recently snubbed by the blond Rapunzel of his dreams: a Hungarian stripper-turned-psychiatrist who'd had quite enough of Malcolm's fawning attention and was capable of spitting poison-tipped barbs through his very soul. Although that astonished him, a certain savagery was what he craved, what he had lacked throughout his boyhood because his mother had been soft as a marshmallow with him. (All this I learned later.)

Meanwhile all of Boulder, especially the Buddhist community, was plunged headlong into "disembodied poetics" mania in the form of the week-long writers' shindig, and Malcolm was proud to attach himself to the "Princess of the Beat Generation." What better way to show up that sharp-toothed vixen Sally?

But I was blindly unaware of this strong undercurrent, and the combination of being thirty, needing a change of scene, the belated sexual awakening, the spirit of the Flatirons looming overhead, and the spectacle of my father being worshipped by hundreds was a lethal one for me. I decided to make Boulder my home.

When Malcolm realized that his not-so-little game with Sally had gone too far, he tried valiantly to dissuade me from moving to Boulder. A Don Juan by nature, he was always up for new affaires, but was careful to cover all bases.

"Wait till October, honey, when I've got my life and my work trip together."

"I don't care about that—I've been poor all my life!" I argued, failing to read between his lines.

"What do you think about monogamy?" he would ask, a playful lilt in his voice, trying to test me, to see if I planned to entrap him.

"I don't know. What about monogamy? Who cares?" I misconstrued his veiled question as being an invitation to monogamy, feeling myself to be the independent agent, exploring new frontiers, willfully casting my fate to the wind with this sudden lock-stock-and-barrel relocation. I had done this sort of thing all my life, so what was there to stop me now?

"August twenty-second—so soon? Well, all right . . . I like to be chased," Malcolm conceded, his little boy's ego puffing up like a frog's throat.

Back in Eugene I had a growing premonition as I packed everything I owned into nine boxes for the Trailways trek: this Boulder chapter of my life could turn out somehow painful . . . certainly intense. But I was ripe for it, whatever it was, and flung myself straight into the flame like a kamikaze moth.

30

The Ceremony of the Red Crown was my true initiation into the Boulder Buddhist community . . . First there was an interminable wait, though nobody seemed quite sure what we were waiting for. We all sat on cushions called *zafus*, staring at the pale green walls of the Elks' lodge (rented specially for the occasion), sweltering in abject patience. By the time even the most orthodox of devotees were getting fidgety, loud chanting began and lamas appeared. One of them donned a red crown of sorts and a procession started. People were lining up as though for communion. One by one, each participant was given a light whisk over the head with a soft floppy broomlike thing and a single string of red yarn was draped over one shoulder.

Some people had so many of these red strings already draped around their necks from previous ceremonies that the bulk would probably keep them warm in winter. The whole to-do ended with sake and more milling about. With all the women dressed up and wearing stockings, and the men in suits, it had the atmosphere of a high-class cocktail party or a gallery opening—the difference was that everyone had left his shoes at the door. Then at the end there was a big crush to see Rimpoche carted off in his limousine.

On the banks of Boulder Creek a few days later, Malcolm and I lay sunning naked on a large whalish rock. Naked, that is, except for our red neck strings. My neck was still sore and stiff from an incident in Denver. I had been seized by a sudden fit of rage when the Trailways baggage man had refused to let me have my boxes, while Malcolm was waiting with the van running, parked illegally. I had let fly a furious string of obscenities at the baggage man— steam that needed venting after a thirteen-hour bus ride from Oregon, perhaps exacerbated by a timely Mars return in 11 degrees of Scorpio. Whatever the reason, the effect had been instant stiff neck, instant karma, and then the Ceremony of the Red Crown for a capper (which Malcolm had obligingly explained had something to do with the three-pronged Trident of Passion, Aggression, and Ignorance—a sort of Holy Trinity, I gathered).

And now, even after three nights of hot tubs and Valium and massages, my neck was still stiff; the red string around it only made it worse. I felt that it was choking me somehow—probably the way a cat feels about wearing a collar. I'd been tugging on it absently for a while, and then, impulsively, I yanked it off and tossed it into the swirling water below us.

"Hey! Whadja do that for?" Malcolm was aghast.

"Seemed like the best thing to do—" I shrugged.

"People usually leave those on for a long time, you know," scolded the well-hung Buddhist plumber condescendingly. "And when they *do* take them off, they're kept in a special place."

"Sorry, it was bothering my neck," replied the writer's daughter. I felt like a naughty little girl, watching the red strand of yarn curl and snake its way slowly down the currents of the creek, past tiny specks of fool's gold lodged in the sediment. What place could be more special than *this?*

Most of September was spent in the sweltering loft of an old carriage house in the alleyway between Spruce and Pearl streets. Malcolm's landlady, Judy, didn't want me staying in his room anymore. The conference had been a different matter. So, there I was until I could find another place: no running water, watching the seconds tick by excruciatingly slowly in the heat, surrounded by my nine boxfuls of junk spread all over the bare wood floor. Piles of letters dating back to Hollywood and before exuded a cloud of spilled jasmine oil. My money was petering out, and the spark that Malcolm had ignited inside me with his savagely refined brand of lovemaking was growing into a four-alarm blaze. My life had literally fallen to pieces. The evidence lay in the ruins all around me. And the magic of the Flatirons was as repelling as it was tantalizing. When I walked aimlessly down Pearl Street toward the mountains I could feel an almost tangible force pushing me away—could almost picture myself being flung bodily from those beautiful green slopes. They looked as unreal as a stage set.

I needed direction. Now that I was here—what? I had failed to think ahead to this point. The only thing I looked forward to, the only thing I found myself longing for dismally every evening, was the distinctive roar of Malcolm's van in the alleyway, followed by his entrance into the loft and then into my body.

Malcolm was an incorrigible tease. I had never known anyone in my life who teased me like he did. In the dark loft, night after night, after he'd been doing whatever it was he did—important manly things like screwing drains in or welding sewer pipes—he liked to pin me down and tickle me till I couldn't catch my breath. I'd laugh and laugh until I thought I'd surely die, but still he wouldn't stop. It was confusing, this type of behavior which was always preliminary to his "tantra." This gave Malcolm an edge, placed him above me in an insidious way. The truth was, he would admit much later, that I reminded him of his kid sister.

Once upon a time on a ranch in Grant's Pass, Oregon . . . Christmas of 1950 . . . there was an infant named Malcolm in a large house, doted on and cooed over by four adults, mother, father, grandmother, and grandfather. Then suddenly, without warning, when he was barely a year old his mother had a baby girl and everything changed drastically. His mother and father moved out of the big house and into a tiny house with little Malcolm and the screaming newcomer. His mother and father started fighting. His grandparents disappeared. The baby sister was now the center of attention and toddler Malcolm found himself totally ignored.

He spent the first ten years of his life teasing his little sister relentlessly until the adults noticed, creating chaos in the Jehovah's Witness household. He nearly drove his gentle mother crazy, so his parents sent him to live with the preacher as punishment. He left home—turned Buddhist—met a woman who reminded him of his father (a strict disciplinarian). She rejected him. Then he met a woman who reminded him of his kid sister. She chased him—and let him tease her.

Once upon a time there was a little girl in New York City with a very beautiful independent mother who took her everywhere on wonderful adventures. The only thing missing from her life was a father. When the little girl finally met her father, he was so wrapped up in his own problems that he didn't even acknowledge her existence. But she idolized him anyway. When she grew up, she thought that all men should be like him—wrapped up in important things, without much time to give to her. So that was the kind of man she found, over and over again. Malcolm was that kind of man.

31

I followed him to the big square building with orange and gold Tibetan designs . . . to the shrine room at Dorje Dzong. Up a quiet carpeted stairway Malcolm sprinted dutifully to the topmost floor. At the rows of sleeping shoes, he slipped his cowboy boots off in a great hurry, afraid to miss something . . . or some*one* perhaps. I took my shoes off and placed them beside his, then entered the spacious room, tiptoeing over polished wood floor, beneath a towering black ceiling. There were a multitude of high arched windows, ornate corners for deities to dwell in glass cases like puppet stages—some with curtains, altars, alcoves, sacred objects. Like a Catholic church, I thought. Then I remembered I was still wearing my gold cross.

Bow at the door, choose a cushion. I sat down on the only black *zafu*, magnetized by its refreshing starkness in the sea of red and yellow ones. Malcolm saw me pick the black one and assumed, as did half a dozen other Tibetan Buddhists, that I had been schooled in Zen.

From where I sat, the jagged belfry of a church across the street was in plain view, as were whirling flocks of pigeons—or were they bats? Seconds and minutes marched by in the heat. Sun streamed a warm rectangle to the wooden floor. I began playing visually with the curly gold leaf of the shrine itself. On my overactive retinal screen a wrecking ball smashed silently into a building, exposing a lone toilet on the seventh floor. *Concentrate on the breath. Label it thinking.*

After trying not to think at all for some time, I came to the conclusion that thinking was more fun. I looked over at Malcolm, wondering if he was able to stop thinking—and I saw his toes: they were touching the meditative girl next to him. Accident? No. They were wiggling, and he had a mischievous glint in his eyes, which were supposed to be "staring into the middle distance." The young woman seemed annoyed yet flattered as she inched away on her cushion.

Bodhisattva my ass. And you know where you can stick that label. So much anger welled up in me that I wondered what was happening to me. Was I going insane? Never had I been so crazy in my life as I'd been since I hit Boulder. . . . But right on the heels of anger came another sensation: I was falling . . . falling backward . . . falling asleep. It had become impossible to stay awake, sitting there in the meditation hall. It was like being on the F train to Queens—a succession of delirious jerking nods claimed me. *Awake. Have to stay awake.* Yes, that was the word Malcolm always used for his butt slapping and teasing rituals. *What does he know about being awake? He must be thinking of that little pamphlet he used to leave on people's doorsteps.* AWAKE. *Nothing but a buzz word for his Buddhist harem.* I had a sudden strong urge to jump up unceremoniously and kick him in the head. . . . Why not just get up and leave? Leave town and go to Santa Fe right now. I used to do things like that in my younger, wilder years.

Cut aggression—work with resistance—address neurosis. The voices of conscience and dogma spoke . . . and then came sarcasm in the same outbreath: *What about* catma? *They say my father couldn't keep his seat, so why should I? Do I even want to?* It was an inner battle.

And then, something different started happening . . . an impossible stretch of time skip-roped by, and I became a breathing statue of wood, limbs intertwined like driftwood in this human cross-legged shape. Discursive thoughts flushed away with each molecule of CO_2—empty yet full. I was surrounded by shimmering space, weightless and perfect. No self. No mind. In the time it took for me to realize what was transpiring, it was gone.

BONNNNNNGGGGG!

The *umse* woke up, too, and sounded his gong.

32

The pumpkin flew through the October twilight and fell to earth
with a round thud—cleft in two on the stone steps of 21 Bluff Street,
scattering seeds into the lawn.

"That's how we used to do it in New York," I said, huffing back
up the steps to Allen, cradling the pumpkin pieces in my arms. He
stood at the door smiling, radiating such warmth. Why had I let so
many years pass between our meetings? Inside, Peter was making
curried chicken and humming to himself in a raspy voice. Finally
I had found sanctuary, and a temporary home, at least, with these
two dear old friends.

"How's your sitting meditation?" asked Allen.

"Hmmm, I really don't know, not so good." I had to be honest,
remembering the other day at Dorje Dzong.

"Well, just keep plugging away," he admonished, going upstairs
with his teapot.

I made pumpkin pie in the kitchen with Peter and we talked about my father, argued about the whereabouts of a certain liquor store in the Lower East Side, shared a bottle of sake. I looked up from the table and noticed a wall calendar for the month of October. On the twenty-first in purple ink someone had drawn an eye with a tear dripping out. . . . October 21 was the day my father died.

"Who drew that eye?" I asked Peter.

"Gregory did, I think, yeah—it was Corso."

The following evening I was alone in the Bluff Street house. As the light waned in the dingy study I stared into the conference poster of my father and the face changed, muted . . . seemed to talk to me. It was the original photo by Arni, much enlarged—dark and grainy.

All alone in that house with the carpets and the television emitting radioactive dust to dust—books asleep on their shelves on the dark side of this moon—ten moons to Halloween. Something like a monkey wrench twists in my isolated psyche . . . a baby girl in Albany, New York, says "Mommy" for the first time. And a thirty-year-old woman in Boulder, Colorado, says "Daddy" for the first time in her life . . . whispers *daddy*—toys with the novel syllables . . . screams DADDY. . . . The word reaches into her throat like a rebel with claws, tearing up her soul—my soul, strangling flesh of his flesh—blood of his blood my blood— screaming in the black mountain silence of Bluff Street revisited visitation. These five letters so unfamiliar to my palate. Can he hear me? I yell louder and louder so that he *will* hear me—all the way from Lowell, Massachusetts under his October in the graveyard earth. But he's not there. Because he's *here* with me, finally, after all this time! He's here in the same house, house of my guardian angels, because I called him with all my might from wherever he was, summoned him from St. Petersburg, Florida—DADDY! The word so many little girls brandish so casually while perched on the laps of all their rock-of-Gibraltar DADDYS. Why not me? Even Ti Jean himself had a daddy—Leo Alcide, who died, and whose last words were "Take care of your mother." I knew what had happened: he was too busy taking care of his mommy to be my DADDY. D A D D Y! It soaks through the firmament of my cells . . . reaching every corner of the house—creeping under the wallpaper, seeping through the floorboards like mist . . . infiltrating the books like ink . . . the whole row of *his* books. Saturated with this primal cry I collapse, with no audience but myself and my father's essence to witness my gesture meant only for him. . . . Lying on the heater grate on the floor, gazing down into the blue glow of the furnace below the foundations of Allen and Peter's old house, I have a talk with my father . . . sit on his lap and listen to his heart beat—his great blue heart and soul beat . . . gaze into his sad blue eyes now on the thirteenth anniversary of his departure from this world.

33

The sour cherry tree behind the house on Pine Street saved my life the following summer. I practically lived under its sturdy, fruit-laden boughs behind the house, safe from fuming buses. Ahhhh, those mornings, those marvelous spells of postawakening when my astral body was still off on some nocturnal rendezvous, and I would pad in simple-footmindedness down the dark Victorian stairs, out through a small kitchen of uncertain territory, and into the backyard herb garden.

Those mornings were quintessential. I could not have survived the summer of '83 without them. Mornings, the cherry tree, and Sitta, Malcolm's Siamese cat. It was really a combination of these three things that kept me sane. Malcolm, however, didn't seem to have any neutral time or space to gather his wits:

Up and at 'em! Rush madly through a shower—a few undigestible bites and gulps—yank on some clothes—zoom away in the blue tool van—race to the shrine room, hair still wet, shirt inside out— He nearly broke his neck in a Buddhist frenzy to arrive at Dorje Dzong in time to sit *still* for three hours!

Didn't I want to come? No, thanks. My meditation was in the garden. Out on the warm back steps was where I did my sitting, in the impossible brilliance of July sun, cup of coffee in hand, watched over by the branches of the sour cherry tree. There, in tranquil verdure, noise from traffic muffled by chlorophyllian muses, I strolled barefoot under the tree, craning my neck to bite the sour cherries off one by one. Standing on tiptoe, the short white terrycloth robe I wore always hiked up to reveal some buttock—though no one could see. Savoring the red tartness of the cherries and feeling the breezes under my robe reminded me that I was alive and free.

Later, twined in summer sheets, thunder from distant clouds taunted the dark amphitheater of my mind, playing back a movie reel of one year earlier, when I had first met Malcolm. July . . . the conference . . . Judy's house . . . the massage . . . thunderstorms electrifying our new romance. But now an emptiness solidified around the bed—a flavorless transparent Jell-o in which I found it hard to move. Where was that electricity now? That chaos which I dreaded most often? In its absence I began to long for it—slam of the van door, socks in little crummy bundles, briefcase dumped loudly by the bed where I'd later stub my toe on it; that raspy laugh brimming with a certain naive machismo; accidental manhood—so infuriating yet so dear. Rough muscular hands, always moving—hammering, wrenching, ripping lace, squeezing, slapping my ass, tangling the telephone cord. Never still, those hands, except in deep sleep or meditation—and even then they twitched.

As I lie in bed I listen to the thunder nearing, sweeping across the Great Plains like great sweeping skirts of giant women with bustles. Sitta jumps up onto the uncannily half-deserted bed and cautiously places her tiny brown paws on my ribs, as though they are stepping stones across a goldfish pond, her luminous blue Siamese eyes gazing ever so steadily into mine. These eyes of hers are soothing to me in much the same way as the sour cherries are. Sapphires of the night, burning bright . . . *Mmrrrp?* she asks, setting down her haunches over my solar plexus, black feline nose two centimeters from human nose. She notices my tears and closes her eyes knowingly for a moment, then licks my chin twice. She decides now is the time to purr.

"Oh, sweetie kit kat, what would I do without you?" I stroke Sitta's small head, reveling in the sensation of having a miniature sphinx vibrating on my chest, so healing to an aching heart, so calming to a troubled mind. We both sleep fitfully in this position.

In the novel unfamiliarity of Faith's bed Malcolm groans. Fully conscious, he wants her to think he is exhausted from love-making. He is basking in the sensation of irresponsibility: a smooth buttery glow in which he thrives. Next morning when he saunters through the front door of the Pine Street house, unsuccessfully trying to hide his beamishness in an orange tank top, I regard him, stock still, my fists clenching and unclenching, undecided as to whether to run to him and embrace or attack him. His hair looks different, fluffier. . . . What did she do to him?

I shut my eyes tightly and see a photo looking me smack in the mind's eye. It's the old black-and-white one I've seen so many times as a child . . . it's in all the biographies—my father, looking for once so healthy and well groomed, in a posed portrait with a pretty blond woman and a pretty little blond girl.

Mommy, we both have dark hair like him. . . . Why is he always in California with the blond women? A voice screamed inside me—then and now and forever. . . .

Upstairs in the cramped boudoir where there was barely enough space to walk around the bed, I did something I had dreamed of doing all my life: with an outcry of pure rage I swept both arms across the cluttered dressertop like Jack Nicholson in *Five Easy*

Pieces—there was "4711" in the catbox, next to a turd and a fifty-dollar bill, rhinestones seeding the floor along with Malcolm's nuts and bolts and pipe fittings, Mount St. Helens's ash all over the purple bedspread, scuba mask outside on the ledge, having flown through the open window—and the jewelry case tinkling tragically out of tune on the floor, its guts exposed. I wondered how I must look to Malcolm, who sat agape on the bed: a mad disheveled woman in a red lace nightie panting with wild rage, scanning the room for something else to demolish—maybe he was next. And maybe I didn't remind him so much of his little sister anymore—perhaps I bore more of a resemblance to Kali, the Hindu goddess of destruction.

34

How on earth had I wound up here in Boulder of all places? So recently I was in Ellensburg, Washington, with Stan. It seemed that I would stay there forever; but then, I had gone to live in Morocco with Bertrand forever too. Forever . . . forever on the move. Perhaps I would never have set foot on these green foothills if it hadn't been for Ken Kesey and his timely visit to the bakery in Eugene. As it turned out, we never even rode to Colorado together as we had planned—instead the Naropa Institute sent us plane tickets and we arrived on separate flights. But I got to see a lot of Kesey during the conference anyway, since he was staying right next door to 813 Maple where I met Malcolm. And what demoniacally divine providence had led me to Malcolm, I often wondered: my life had evidently been too easy so far, and the powers that be were shifting the balance by steering me into this man. Someone who could make my life supremely difficult. Someone to tease me and inconvenience me and drive me to assert myself. It had taken fifteen months of Boulder and Malcolm to get to this combustion point, and now my kamikaze moth wings were about to catch on fire.

But besides this passionate love-hate thing I had going with Malcolm, being in Boulder and in contact with Naropa had put me in touch with a whole new realm of writers and poets from all over the world. And in October of '83 I was invited by my German publisher to go to Europe to do a string of readings. Ironically, just before I was set to leave for Germany, Malcolm and I were getting along better than ever.

October 12. Malcolm drove me to Paramount Drive, to the house of a certain Milo Trump, another author, also a Buddhist, who had hired Malcolm to work on his plumbing. Their relationship was a strange one, I thought. They were always goading each other with a cynical one-upmanship like rival little boys.

A Cadillac limousine was waiting in front when we pulled up. The license plate, white on green for Colorado, said PADMA 17.

"Ahh. Padma Limo, the Buddhist company. That Milo's got class!" Malcolm yelled in the direction of the house, from which a darkly handsome man walked briskly with too many suitcases.

Milo cocked his head to one side and chuckled, winking a luminous brown eye. "You look lovely, sweetheart."

"Thanks, honey," cooed Malcolm, getting out of the blue van with my bags.

"Not *you*, shithead!" Milo called from inside the trunk.

The chauffeur looked back and forth at them with uncertain smiles, a bit nonplussed by this exchange. Now that the initial formalities were out of the way, Malcolm shook Milo's hand. "Well, have a good trip, man. Take care of her, you hear?"

"Yeah, I'll take better care of her than you do—that's for sure!" laughed Milo, slapping him on the back.

I kissed Malcolm good-bye and bounced myself in next to Milo on the plush seat. All at once a wave of exhaustion came over me. After all the preparations—the going-away party, the transatlantic telegrams, the last-minute mending on the lining of my mouton lamb coat—I felt for a brief moment intimidated by the thought of all of Europe, stretching for miles out there somewhere, all the yet unseen railway stations, gray boulevards, steeples, forests, people with and without cigarettes. I was a little girl again, and I didn't want to go to school. It was the first attack of agoraphobia I'd had in my adult life.

Flouncing my skirt out from under Milo's leg, I quickly buzzed down the push-button window to blow a kiss to Malcolm, who suddenly seemed more desirable, now that I was leaving the hemisphere altogether. The huge automobile wheezed and clicked. Our driver had left the headlights on and now the battery was dead. But our knight in dull blue armor hadn't sped away yet, thank Buddha. Malcolm was ready and willing with the jumper cables. This gave him an opportunity to play Mechanical Savior, his favorite role.

Thanks to this false-alarm farewell, we made it to Denver and Stapleton Airport just under the wire. Then while we were in Manhattan for a two-hour stop-over, I had time to burn as Milo did manic business dealings from his father's penthouse on Park Avenue. I ran around with customary exhilaration on my old turf, bantering with the Arabs who had uncannily replaced Puerto Ricans in the uptown bodegas, searching for a decent Danish, inhaling great gasps of familiar long-lost manhole steam, pretzel smoke, and subway breezes, rushing along in the never-ending aerobics class of wide-load pavement, sidewalks that were wider than most *streets* in Europe . . . secretaries prancing, businessmen cantering, young messenger boys at full gallop on rusty bicycles backward through midtown yellow taxi herds—too much to absorb in a million years, let alone two lousy *hours*.

Many hours and a few flight years later after a turbulent gin-filled night over the North Atlantic, dawn began to seep through the portholes of our tireless bird. Finally I saw Earth below . . . the color green . . . lots of it—testimony to a good deal more moisture than one finds in the American West at this time of year. And little whitish-gray clusters neatly arranged on this green carpet. Then nothing. No clusters at all for a while—just green carpet. Suddenly—another group of structures. How different this was from the helter-skelter scattering of buildings seen in aerial views of the U.S. Here, it was as if some giant neurotic child had been playing with blocks, but he was careful to keep them corralled into tidy enclosures so as not to mess up the living room floor. Whereas the American child was a creative slob, scattering his blocks willy-nilly, wherever there was an open space (and Lord knows there's no shortage of *space* in *his* living room).

I had never before flown so far east at once, and this was my first run-in with true jet lag. It was Columbus Day, and here I was discovering the Old World. "How backward of you, my dear," I scolded myself, staggering past outdoor stands of German sausage. A galaxy of aromas spilled through holes in my etheric body— bratwurst, knockwurst, thiswurst, thatwurst. . . . My previous infatuation with New York hot dogs was quickly paling. Smell seemed to be the only one of my five senses still functioning as I sleepwalked through the Frankfurter *Buchmesse* like a narcoleptic zombie.

That first day of the Frankfurt Book Fair, I couldn't even focus on the shiny displays of books in the mammoth Orwellian buildings. And as it turned out, Milo and I had nowhere to stay. The visiting throngs of 1983 had been underestimated, and all the hotels within a twelve-kilometer radius were packed. So we spent most of the day in the housing office, waiting for *zimmers* to be arranged for us somehow, listening to our energetic hosts yammering away in soothing *Deutsch* through copious clouds of cigarette smoke as they decided what was to be done with us. How ironic: I was fascinated by every detail but couldn't keep my eyes open. Fearful of seeming ungrateful, I would jerk myself awake for a moment or two, mumble something unintelligible, and then crash back to the land of Nod. But they must have seen many a wasted wayfarer from the West at this cultural crossroads.

The following day I was back to abnormal after a whole night's slumber in heavenly goosedown comforters. At first when I left the States, I'd entertained some silly notion about giving up caffeine and alcohol after a several-month-long poison spree. But the atmosphere of the book fair was one of such intense celebration fused with frenetic business deals, that to refuse wine or beer or coffee here was about as unheard-of as refusing salt in a Bedouin's tent.

Passing through the guarded gates to the fairgrounds each morning, showing our orange PRESSE cards to the dangerously bored-looking militia with their khaki uzis, I couldn't help but think of Malcolm. His built-in pattern of behavior was to make a spectacle, to call attention to himself. Fine and dandy in the good ole US of A where he could talk his way out of most any situation. But *here*. . . . Cruelly, I found myself savoring an imaginary scenario: Malcolm had made a scene and was being roughed up. I waved good-bye to him as he was carted off, kicking and screaming, by the guards.

35

Amsterdam. Dawn in the red-light district. I had made the mistake of following Milo into a labyrinth of narrower-than-narrow alleyways. He wandered from window to pink lace window like a little boy in a candy store. But Milo was a discerning little boy—he knew what he liked. Only the best sour lemon balls or butterscotch jawbreakers would do, or maybe, just maybe, a banana marshmallow in a pinch. He was in search of the perfect blond.

Thinking we were just out for a stroll, I had worn my black suede boots with three-inch spike heels. They were definitely not the thing for Amsterdam's deeply rutted, highly irregular cobblestones. I was twisting my ankles at every other step, wondering if I would ever walk normally again. But at the same time I was keeping ten paces behind Milo at his request, like an Arab wife, so the red light girls would think he was alone. I couldn't lose track of him either, because he had the keys to the hotel room—and he was swallowed up by one dungeonlike alley after another.

"Milo, there's one! You just passed a nice blond. What was wrong with her?"

"Legs not long enough!" he called back bluntly.

"Ow! Jesus," I gasped, twisting my ankle again. "There's one with long legs."

"Too fat!"

"You know, you're a hard man to please." My voice echoed in the crepuscular canals.

"Yeah, I know," he said proudly.

I stopped to rest my throbbing ankles for a moment, and quickly discovered that to be stationary was perhaps even more hazardous: men began to approach me, thinking I was a streetwalker, and the ladies framed in pink lace glared daggers at me from their display windows.

"Boy—I'm glad I'm not married to you," I panted, catching up to my inattentive escort.

"Come on, let's catch a cab back to the hotel," I insisted.

"Okay, I guess it's just you and me again, sweetheart," Milo sighed disappointedly for the cabby's entertainment as we climbed in.

"You mean you'll settle for a chocolate-covered cherry?"

Next morning, Milo and I sat at a table in the breakfast room of the Jan Luyken hotel, mildly amazed to find ourselves in Amsterdam together—both acutely aware of the strangeness of everything, starry-eyed and weary all at once, as we soaked in the alien forms of mundaneness like sponges from another world. We toyed with the awkward tubular containers and array of cold cuts heaped up on a tray . . . when all of a sudden, a very unusual being appeared.

He was tall, yet somehow unfinished in his build, like a giant adolescent, with a potbelly under a bright red T-shirt that advertised MONTANA . . . blond, mustachioed . . . deeply disturbed. This obviously American creature sat down at the table adjoining ours, muttering something about a bottle of whiskey, and buried his head in his hands. *Suffering from jet lag, among other things,* I quickly surmised.

Polite humans that we were, we pretended to ignore the problematic newcomer, busying ourselves instead with the oddly weak version of Dutch coffee and the stale bread that could be happily camouflaged in a galaxy of preserves and soft butter. But it was difficult, at least for me, to ignore this guy in the Montana T-shirt. Somehow, I felt a kinship with him and his inexplicable suffering. I could feel how complex he was inside—and I could sense that all his wires were tangled.

He began to talk, to no one in particular.

"I was walking through Harlem," he began, quite naturally, as if he'd known us all his life, "and this black guy said, 'Hey, you in de Elmo Fudd hat!' "

At this point, by way of demonstration our new friend pulled something black out of his pants pocket and slapped it atop his fair head. It was sort of pillbox shaped with a pom-pom in the middle.

"Well, I turned around, in mortal terror, and smiled at him of course. And then his buddy said to him, '*Man,* leave de dude alone—anyone who wears an Elmo Fudd hat is awright wi' me!' So, you see, this hat saved my life today—or was it yesterday morning? No . . . I think it was tomorrow, as a matter of fact. Oh, hell, I don't know. . . . Goddamnit, isn't there any *whiskey* in this place??"

This was Richard Brautigan. Like me, he was here for the Poetry Festival at the Milky Way, or Melkweg—a notorious old place that had been a hangout for beatniks, then hippies, a truly avant-garde theater-gallery-café for several decades. There had been a major metamorphosis in recent years: like grasshoppers becoming locusts, it seemed the old bohemians had turned into punks. But appearances were deceiving. For in actuality the beatniks had just gotten older; the hippies had either dissolved or turned themselves inside out, into anachronistic parodies of their former selves. And these wild Euro punks were a totally new and different breed . . . risen from the ashes of the atomic age—immune to everything under the sun.

Brautigan finally managed to scare up some whiskey that morning, and wound up getting Milo thoroughly plastered, putting him out of commission for the rest of the day. I walked into the hotel room at 2 PM to find them both passed out on the floor. I took this opportunity to explore Amsterdam on my own—but this time in *real* shoes.

This city gave me new perspectives on my own hometown, which, after all, had barely missed being Nieuw Amsterdam. It turned its dusky facets to me, one by one, like a rare old amethyst. I felt that I knew this place, with so many leaning brick buildings propped up with poles, and mad yellow trams that threatened to run me down. I found Indonesian cafés everywhere, and fabulous chocolates intricate enough to make Godiva look sick. Just as I had grown accustomed to *strasses*, now I found myself delightfully lost among *straats* and canals. My wanderings led me to the Van Gogh museum. Disappointed to hear that *Starry Night* was in New York, I went upstairs and stared fixedly at *Lemons* for half an hour. The thick yellow swirls of paint so close to my nose were swirling me back to the Yugoslavian freighter, re-creating the pitch and roll of those nights spent in the berth of cabin #13 hugging huge pillows, gazing into the tiny reproduction of this very same painting.

Back outside in the crazed bustle of screeching trams, I set off in search of the Melkweg. In desperation I asked some fellows in odd brown uniforms, only to discover that they were Hungarian poets who were also here for the festival and spoke no English. They were lost, also looking for the Melkweg, and since I spoke no Hungarian we had a great time finding the place together. We arrived in the dingy canal street amid throngs of spiked heads and studded leather and pink chrome and green chains.

Richard Brautigan was inside, still drinking. In the three days before the reading he must have drunk six quarts of whiskey. I watched him carrying on and felt a poignancy for him—not unlike what I had felt for my father. By the time he was scheduled to read, he had drunk himself stone sober, and I think he was terrified. He went on stage before a mixed audience of Europeans—Dutch, German, Italian, French, Danish—punks and generic bohemians of all sorts. He went on with the same attitude I'd seen in the breakfast room the morning of his arrival: hangdog, terminally sad. He belatedly began to tell a story.

It was all about an ant—a black ant who was making his way perilously underneath the black shoes of a line of people at a funeral for a Japanese man. He went on and on, quietly, morosely, about the ant, which kept barely escaping being crushed by the soles of shuffling shoes. The audience was riveted—you could hear a safety pin snap in a punk's ear. Then, after five minutes, without warning, he stopped.

"MORE!" roared the audience. They began chanting "BRAUTIGAN" in a motley mix of accents. They were outraged and wanted to see and hear more. Brautigan meekly apologized. He shrugged his narrow shoulders and said he didn't have any more. Then, as an afterthought it seemed, he explained that the Japanese man whose funeral the ant was walking through would have been insulted if he had read any more, that the Japanese like things simple—short and sweet, like haiku. Then he left.

That was the first and last time I saw Richard Brautigan . . . strange sweet fellow with so much unseen trauma inside. One year later he was found dead in his cabin in Livingston, Montana, having shot himself.

Bathed in blue dreamlight onstage at the Milky Way, I read an elegy to my long-lost daughter Natasha. It was a last-minute decision, and the intensely tropical flavor of the poem which I had written in Mexico at age sixteen cast a spell on everyone, including me.

Back at the Jan Luyken later I saw an elegant older man in a gray suit and hat sitting in the middle of a crowd of young admirers. He reminded me of an old gentle gray tomcat, and I wanted to go over and pet him. He was well protected, though, this dignified feline . . . and before I had a chance to get to know him, a bodyguard spirited William Burroughs away for a nap.

That was the eve of departure from Holland, for both Milo and myself. Milo would go to England the next morning, and I had been offered a ride to Paris with some Dutch journalists. But that very night, just as I was going to bed, there was a phone call for me . . . a man who said we had never met, who spoke frantically, breathlessly, with a terrifying urgency—said he had to see me. From the very first moment, his voice put me off. But I tried to be civil, and said he could meet me tonight briefly if he wanted, downstairs in the lounge. He was three hundred miles away and if he drove very fast he could be here in two hours! No, in that case, I said, some other time because I would be leaving for Paris in the morning. Then he could drive me there! He insisted with desperation. By then I was getting mad. I told him he could reach me at a certain number on the twenty-fifth in Tübingen, and even that was probably not a wise thing to do. Then I had to hang up on him.

It was hard to sleep, just knowing that there was this maniac out there somewhere who wanted to meet me so badly—I feared I had made a terrible mistake in giving him the number in Tübingen . . . I drifted into a disturbed delirium, trying to think up ways of evading him once I got there. But in the morning he was the farthest thing from my mind.

36

I arrived in Paris on October 21, the anniversary of my father's death. I cashed in all of my colorful Dutch guilders for francs and went right to a fruit stand, so hungry I couldn't think straight—I tried to buy a mango. The Parisian fruit vendor immediately began giving me hell about something, and I decided right then and there that I would prefer to speak Spanish instead of English, since French was impossible. I hadn't had time to identify all the denominations of francs, either, and was dropping them to the floor. Then he really started in on me, screaming something derogatory about pesetas. Normally I would have reciprocated with a stream of curses à la Nuevo Yorkeño, but at that point I was so confused and disoriented that I left the fruit stand without even flipping him off.

Out I went into the hustle bustle near the Pompidou Center's atrocious blue pipes, dragging luggage and trying to eat this turpentine horror of an unripe mango, getting strings caught in my teeth and searching high and low for a taxi. It took me a while to realize that there were throngs of taxi vultures grabbing all the taxis a block ahead before they even had a chance to pass me—so after getting much more aggressive than I wanted to, I finally caught one, the interior of which reeked of dog—not one of my favorite fragrances.

"Dix-neuf rue de l'Université, s'il vous plaît," I said in my best *français* to the lady driver and her pet dog, which rode beside her in the front seat. We proceeded to plow through the Paris pedestrians and it occurred to me that a cattle guard would be quite handy here. On the Rive Gauche we went down rue Jacob and rue de l'Université . . . and I saw number 18. I asked her to leave me off there and she protested. Naturally I assumed 19 wasn't far from 18. I convinced her that right here was fine, suffocating as I was from essence of pooch. Out once more in the fresh clear lead smog, I walked across the street to find—guess again—number 36! Well, what did I expect to find? *Am I nuts?*

I marched on and on and on. . . . The numbers went down, then up, then down. There didn't seem to be any rhyme or reason here. I went into little courtyards and asked washerwomen very nicely, *"Où est dix-neuf?"* But not a soul had a clue. As a last resort I went into a corner café and asked to use the phone—but the proprietor wouldn't let me! I asked if he'd ever heard of Editions Denoël. No. Never. I began to feel utterly jinxed; I felt as though Paris symbolized my father and he wouldn't listen to me, didn't care! I shook with frustration and rage and had trouble holding back tears. I suppose it was this spectacle which wasn't meant to be a spectacle that changed my luck. Someone called the number for me, head shaking in pity and disgust, and in a few moments the secretary of Denoël came to rescue me: how could I have possibly missed it? Yes, how stupid of me not to know that 19 comes right after 42!

Once I got up to my French publisher's, the Twilight Zone flavor of the initial Paris blast began to dissolve, thank God. My editor took me out to dinner that evening to a Spanish restaurant and told me something that was rather amazing to hear: that my father had experienced a real nightmare when he first came to France, that, coincidentally, he had felt the same frustration as I did—for different reasons, though, he being a Breton and a Cannuck, and speaking Quebecois, which might as well have been a foreign language as far as the snotty Parisians were concerned.

I got a room in the Hotel Lenox, just down the block from Denoël and, after sniffing out the place like a cat, I met some likable and even a few lovable Parisians. Then things began to change. I strolled along the Seine, fed pigeons with winos, window-shopped on rue Jacob . . . and somehow, the sight of Notre Dame in the distance didn't attract me the way I had expected it would. I wound up instead at l'Abbaye Saint-Germain. Following my deeply buried Catholic roots in a trance, my footsteps led me up the marble stairs and I responded blindly to an embryonic urge. I felt as if I were a fourteen-year-old French girl attending Catholic school in Paris. There were some definite similarities to New York here, though I couldn't quite pinpoint them—a certain set of smells that filled the air with P.S. 61 and St. Mark's Church . . . Washington Square . . . the Statue of Liberty. . . .

In I went, into the flickering sanctuary, a devout little heathen returning to the fold, back from the war of the world. To my right as I entered was a statue of Saint Germain, surrounded by glowing white candles.

I decided I would light a candle for my father now. An ornate metal box, the sort I used to rob money from in New York churches, had a simple, hand-lettered sign with prices of candles: five francs, four, or three, in order of thickness. I had only three francs with me, so it would have to be a skinny one. Besides, Saint Germain was watching and so was my father—so I never even considered stealing a fat candle. The one I got was so thin at the bottom that it was difficult to stick it onto the little metal spike without breaking it. I tried and tried, and the wax whittled away and it got shorter and shorter. Then I got an idea: why not remedy the problem by heating the base of my father's candle on another's flame? As I did this I wondered what effect it might be having.

Could it be that Dominique LaSalle, a seventy-nine-year-old woman confined to a wheelchair on, let's say, rue St-Denis, was having a sudden visitation from the late Jean-Louis Kérouac . . . all because his skinny three-franc candle was being heated from below by the strong flame of her fat five-franc wick?

As I envisioned this scenario, a drop of hot white wax dripped from my father's candle onto the navy blue linen of my right jacket sleeve—there to stay. Finally, I got the poor candle, or what was left of it, to stay, slightly askew, on its prong.

"There you are, Jack, I mean Daddy, which I never had the pleasure of calling you when . . ."

All at once the flames were smearing wildly, melting into a bronze underwater blaze. I blotted my eyes with the wax-stained sleeve and stepped back out into the sun.

37

Wandering back through ritzy rue Jacob, past glittering shop windows, amid throngs of Parisians dodging piles of poodle poop which seemed to have been placed strategically like land mines along the sidewalks, I began to feel at home in the Rive Gauche. Having prowled the neighborhood, I sauntered into the lobby of the Hotel Lenox that afternoon.

There had been a change of shifts at the desk while I was out: the Green-Eyed One was gone now, replaced by a dark, strangely animated fellow with high cheekbones. I approached the front desk. "*Vingt-cinq, s'il vous plaît,*" I said, holding out my palm for the key. The new desk clerk absently pulled my key out of its cubbyhole, spoke to one hotel guest in Spanish, and answered a beeping phone in French. I leaned against the cool marble and reached for the key in his hand. He shot me a playful twinkly look and actually *withheld* my key.

All sorts of thoughts flew through my head then. I was quite tired from walking and had planned on going upstairs for a nap, but I was already hypnotized by his unusual behavior—the audacity of this fellow!

"Are you Canadian?" he asked, bringing me up short.

"Well, French Canadian—half, that is," I offered, my head cocked to one side, full of questions.

"Bet you can't guess what I am!" he said with such unbridled parochial enthusiasm that I felt transported back to sixth grade. All of a sudden I wasn't the least bit tired. Now I was burning with curiosity to guess where on earth this fascinatingly bold, friendly, presumptuous chap who still hadn't given me my key was from.

"Hmmm . . . let's see . . . Filipino?"

"Nope."

Okay, I thought. *Anyone who says "nope" like that has to have spent a great deal of time in the States.*

"Puerto Rican?"

"You're getting warmer."

I felt as if I were playing twenty questions with my childhood sweetheart, Peter Bunks, in upstate New York. This was fun. *And he speaks Spanish and French, too.*

"Algeria?"

He shook his head no. "Give up? Honduran Indian and Basque."

"You're right, I never would have guessed!"

Now he handed me number 25 over the cool marble of the desk, intentionally ignoring some other guests who wanted their keys. A static moment of flirtation ensued. His black eyes glittered and I wavered.

"Do you know where the word *lady* came from?" he asked, resuming his magicianlike tricks with languages and keys and phones.

"Old English, I think."

"Yes! Very good! Old English for loaf maker, *hlaefdige*, and the lord or laird was the loaf *keeper.*"

"So, the queen is a great loaf maker!" As we played our game, I wondered how we had clicked into such an instantaneously compatible repartee, especially under such improbable circumstances. I dallied at the desk, talking with my new friend for an hour or more, trading word origins and playing fascinating mental games. We were like honeybees doing intricate wing dances for each other to describe where the honey is. He told me about the word *albatross*, and how the Portuguese had heard the Arabs saying *Al qatraz*, then misconstrued it; I told him how *tuxedo* had come from an Algonquin word for *wolf*, and how an apron only a short time ago was really a napron; we took apart the roots of *sabotage* and sifted through *scrutiny* like Roman ragpickers.

After a while, my exhaustion came back full force, and I had to tear myself away from my brilliant acquaintance. Trudging somewhat reluctantly up the stairs to my room, my mind was spinning with a million wondering ifs. . . . What if I didn't have to go back to Germany early tomorrow morning? What might happen then? But there was no time and no way to find out. The possibilities would have to remain locked in a parallel universe—untapped. Perhaps that was just as well, since his name was Miguel, and I had a history of bad luck with Miguels. I was sure that at first we would get along famously, if our relationship had a chance to get off the ground. But then what? Where would the inevitable conflict start? How would it be manifested? It was fascinating to turn these thoughts over and over in my mind—like turning a sour lemon candy over with my tongue. I lay down on the tight, crisply made bed and daydreamed for a spell, then picked up the distinctive gray Parisian phone and called the desk.

"Hello, this is room 25. I need a wake-up call at five AM."

"Hi, room 25, I recognized your voice. Say, do you know where the term *gringo* came from?"

"No, I can't imagine. Why don't you tell me?" I said, pulling the receiver under the covers with me and preparing for an entertaining bedtime story.

"Well, in Mexico, in Maximilian's army there were troops of Irish soldiers, and when they marched they would sing a little song to remind themselves of Ireland because they were homesick. It went, 'Green grows the grass in Ireland,' et cetera. When the Mexicans saw these guys march they'd say, 'Oh, there go those *greengrows* again.' "

"Amazing. And *greengrows* became *gringos*," I said, genuinely pleased to be sung lullabyes over the phone, snuggling into the bed and wishing the desk clerk were in bed with me too instead of just the phone.

I slept fitfully that night, intensely aware of the time limit I was under. And my subconscious didn't trust the fellow downstairs to wake me in time. I awoke just before five, packed quickly in the Paris predawn, and descended the twisty stairwell to the marble lobby. There he was, lying under a blanket on a couch, his complex mind presumably at rest for a change. The little brass clock alarm went off, and an arm shot out from under the blanket, knocking the clock across the shiny empty floor of the lobby. I retrieved it for him as he leapt up guiltily and greeted me.

"Ah—*bonjour, madame!* Good morning."

"*Buenos dias, Señor.*"

The linguistics major from the Sorbonne called a cab for me, and we exchanged last-minute addresses and phone numbers, neither of us awake enough to cook up witty wordicisms so early in the morning. The cab arrived too soon. I felt a strange force pulling me to it—something like the hands of Fate, an inexorable tide that made my feet walk out onto the street against my will. Would we ever meet again? Choices. Footsteps and miles. An affaire in microcosm.

38

Gare du l'Est . . . the glossy orange trains bundled together like
fat worms for fish bait. I raced to catch one, zipping past women
walking herds of poodles tangled up in leashes, bored gendarmes,
and pissing punks, glad to be moving again. Strasbourg . . . Stutt-
gart . . . Tübingen . . . the prevailing magnetic pull here was toward the east. I remembered that relentless momentum in South
America, down, down, down, to the south. But now here I was,
reeling ever eastward, feeling a certain relief to be returning to
Germany. Some crazy voice deep in my soul kept saying, "Ahh,
back to the Fatherland." But on second thought, maybe it wasn't
so crazy. After all, being such a Heinz 57, how could I know which
voice was which? It must have been my one-eighth Dutch talking—
my mother's father's mother to be exact.

In Tübingen I stayed at a tiny *Gusthaus* where hefty young girls
had pillow fights as they cleaned the rooms. Wandering through

narrow twisty cobblestone streets, I could almost feel the cramped human psyche of old that had built these snail-shell wonders; it was a little like going back to kindergarten and sitting in a tiny chair again. I kept wondering if that nameless maniac was going to call again. Why had I done such a stupid thing as give him the phone number here? But to my glad surprise he never called at all.

After a brief placid vision of two swans floating on the green glass of the river Neckar, a tall castle in the distance, I went ever eastward—to the manure-laden fields of Bavaria. Ulm . . . Augsburg . . . Rettenbergen. This land was weaving a spell of lethargy over me. For three days all I could do was sleep. Sleep, then call my mother across the globe . . . then eat *blaukraut* and *pflaumkuchen*, then go back to sleep.

But in Munich I woke up again. And when I met Martin—"the man from TV"—I had a strong premonition that something very unusual would happen with him in Berlin—and it would have nothing to do with TV. In a sort of car pool called *der Mitfahr Zentrale* I rode with two Germans and a Turk all the way from Munich through Nürnberg and endless gray snaking autobahns in the rain to Berlin. At first there was silence in the car, but by the time we got to Checkpoint Charlie and handed all four passports through the window in a stack, we shared a common bond: a little bubble of transitory family, we sensed the danger at large.

Somewhere in the middle of the DDR, dark, windy, and alien, we stopped to find a toilet. I walked across a crumbling old bridge over the East German highway to a strange gray building with bare light bulbs and a big heap of coal bricks glistening in the questionable night. A wet rag had been stretched across an iron grating in the floor for some obscure washerwoman's reason—and there she was, the keeper of the toilets herself, lurking in the adjacent room in babushka and more rags. Unlike those in Deutschland West, this one wasn't demanding *pfennigs*—just hovering in limbo between helpfulness and hostility. Sluggish flies abounded, despite the apparently pristine gray stalls where amazing gray toilet paper hung on industrious twine. Not a speck of graffiti *here*. And the toilet paper was strong—kind of like seersucker cardboard that has been through a washing machine three times. I kept some in my pocket for a souvenir but later accidentally threw it away.

After enduring more customs inspection, we entered West Berlin. There we were in that city of surprising color and brightness in the middle of the night. Not a claustrophobic prison surrounded by forbidding wastelands as I had expected, but an uncanny oasis of culture shining like an emerald in a mud puddle. I felt like Dorothy entering Oz. Lots of drunks made me a tad nervous when I was cast upon subways and unknown streets to cower in bright yellow phone booths. The Turk came with me part of the way before he had to move on. He waited while I called Martin, and upon hearing the busy signal, shook his head and said, *"Besetzt."*

Martin's number was *besetzt* for a long time, so I hailed a cab. The driver was a Jew who spoke good English; in fact, he bore a striking resemblance to Allen Ginsberg. All day long in the car pool I had been practicing my pronunciation of Martin's address: *"Schlesische Strasse zweiunddreissig."* But now when I finally had to say it, I tripped over my tongue. After a disorienting ride that wound through many strangely surreal boulevards and alleyways, we arrived at number 32—in a neighborhood as sleazy as the Lower East Side of Manhattan. I walked up to the door while the driver waited, and I was greeted by a double row of doorbells. Lots of names, but no Fohman. I'm stumped. What do I do, ring all of them?

I call the cabby over to help me, to speak German through the voice box: *"Herr Ploog da?"* But no one seems to know the name. Maybe he just moved in. Or he's visiting. Perhaps he's not even supposed to be here! I try calling him again; the nearest phone booth is three blocks away. Four young men, toppling drunk, reel past me. This is a real party town—I get the feeling that there's no sense of time here in West Berlin.

The cab driver is very sympathetic. He drives me back to the bright yellow phone booth. By now I've memorized Martin's number, and I'm getting quite adept at using the Berlin pay phones. It's still *besetzt!* Seven times more—*besetzt*. We return to the building, and I'm starting to feel a bit paranoid. What a place to be lost! This is the kind of thing one's mother is always worried will happen. . . .

Back to the bells. This time Eli (the Allen-like cabbie and I were on a first-name basis by now) takes a meditative look at them and picks at random. *"Herr Ploog da?"* he ventures—to which a flood of affirmation bursts forth from the crackly *Deutschephone*. I can't believe my luck—this kindly, balding, grandfatherly cabdriver pressed the right bell on his first try. He must be one of my guardian angels.

And here's Saint Martin, bounding springily down the stairs, full of youthful energy. He picks up my heavy bags as if they were featherweight and kisses me, saying in a delightful Bavarian lilt, "I don't believe you found this place!"

We run together up six flights to the top floor of a beautiful spacious loft. Five people are seated at a large table when we enter, two men and three women. They greet me so warmly that I feel I've stumbled upon a gathering of my old friends. The atmosphere is one of magical ease. Even so, I am sharply aware of the ratio of males to females, and I wonder if I'm upsetting the balance. I put out feelers, but detect no vibes of resentment. I find these Europeans to be amazingly open-hearted. They seem to have so much to think about—real substantial stuff—that there's no time for petty details.

Inge makes me some curried cauliflower, and there's good Spanish wine on the table—candles burning way down. Heidi hangs up the phone and comes to apologize for keeping the line tied up, with a real blush on her face—something I've rarely seen. Dinner having dissipated without formality, Martin shows me the loft. We dance, and he lifts me way up, like a long-lost brother. The other loft mates are genuinely glad for him. He shows me his bed from Afghanistan, all woven onto a pole frame. Here's a logistics problem: he wants to move it into the back room, but can't do it without either chopping a bigger doorway or taking the whole bed apart. Ahh, no matter— it will just have to stay where it is for now.

While still in Bavaria, lazing in the doldrums of fertilized hills, I had already imagined what this place in Berlin would be like. Martin had told me in Munich that it was close to the Wall, so I knew that from the start. But the feeling of the place, the windows and which way they face, the location of the bed, even the color scheme, lots of pastels and beige, all made up an image that was nearly perfect. Never before had my preconception of a place turned out to be so accurate. Where in the blue swirls of my Breton psyche was there a bubble reserved for Berlin? A little crystal ball the size of a dewdrop, planted before birth perhaps, it was growing rapidly now, almost life-sized.

As I stand in the entranceway to the living room area, the visual perspective burns onto my retinal screen in Cinemascope: the chess-board of straw mats stretching for yards across the floor, the huge old blocky desk from some Nazi's war office, sooty magnificence of towering unbombed windows one-and-a-half men high—even the CLANK and GROINK of ironworkers below slaving away at the bottom of the airshaft. It feels like a foreshadowing, some sort of clairvoyance—a scene not yet actualized. But it is happening *Now*. "So, what do you want to do?" he asks, doing a somersault on the mats.

"Gee—I really don't know. Don't care, either. It's just fine being here with you," I say, leaping across the chessboard.

"Well, at any rate, milady, I'm at your service! We could go out drinking and dancing. Berlin never stops, you know."

"Yes, I got that impression."

"Or if you want to sleep, there's my bed—or that other one or that one over there."

"Oh, thank you, kind sir, but I really couldn't sleep now, I'm much too—" He kisses my hand and I curtsey. We are like marionettes, falling in and out of roles, playing people of different times . . . adjusting ourselves to each other . . . turning new facets this way and that to catch the light just right.

"Hey, whaddayou say we go to a late movie!" All of a sudden Martin is an American boy-next-door type—practicing the wide-mouthed drawl of the West.

"Oh, Rhett, Ah don't know—Ah feel so tahred!" I feign a faint, knowing he'll catch me.

We go on like this, with the uncanny unspoken assurance that anything goes, all is possible, *alles ist gut.* In deep shadow beneath those great windows we lie, hours later, happily wasted from theatricals. Same earth, same sky, on the other side of a huge global room. Base rumbles and lapidary modulations of The Police fill the shimmering darkness of the loft on so real a night in Eastern Europe, just twelve meters from the Wall—so close that we can hear trees rustling on the other side.

"Bed's too big without you . . . without yoooooo!" The penetrating cadence of these flaxen-haired boys would ever afterward sweep me back to Berlin and the loft. And such a bed, this Afghani tangle of colorful ropes and poles. Earlier I'd cat-walked along the edge as he lay there and admired my balance which seemed to manifest itself for his eyes only. Something was happening—my blood was undergoing a transformation. Could all this be happening in the same lifetime?

We lie in utter freedom smack dab in the middle of a fascist police state—yet there's more freedom of the soul than I ever remember feeling in the U.S. Why? We're intertwined sweetly . . . human beings after all. This could go on forever. The morning sun could roll over us after streaming across the Soviet steppes, illuminating too many cobblestones for the mind to fathom. Coal barges, cabbage fields—steeple spires divested of their crosses . . .

"I'll be wrapped around your finger. . . ." Slipping through worlds of sound and touch—a melding of body and soul—right here where so much suffering took place not so long ago. A movie reel of Claire Bloom and Richard Burton scrambling over barbed wire in searchlight halos flashes black and white in my imagined sight. A child's query from age five creeps in: Are we blood brothers?

39

November first, All Saints' Day. Dawn spreads over us like soft butter and Martin suggests, "Shall we go to East Berlin today?" Making it sound like a bloody amusement park. And with *him*, I'm sure it will be. We skip-run down the stairs the way I used to as a kid in New York. And then it strikes me—*West Side Story*. That's what it feels like here! The unexpected sudden romance, the blackened brick of inner-city tenements, the high level of exhilaration in the air . . . Where are the Jets?

We made one stop before going east that morning, at Kreuzberg, a neighborhood of condemned buildings inhabited by squatters. We visited a punk couple, sobered by the birth of their baby. They occupied a sixth-floor walk-up right next to some heavy demolition. It was terribly noisy and we had to scream to be heard as they heated formula on a hot plate. They have to sneak in and out the back door so no one will know they live there. It reminded me of my own childhood in the slums. I told them this as Martin translated, and they were aghast, disbelieving—an American girl, living like *this*. I was happy to enlighten them on this point.

Running by the Wall, admiring the great graffiti, we saw a platform and climbed up. On top we could see the guard towers on the other side. Almost instantly two guards lifted binoculars to their eyes to check us out. Being such theatrical fools, we decided to put on a show for them—a passionate kiss. And then, with a kind of elated fear nipping at our heels like the fear of boogeymen under the bed, we jumped down and danced past Turks selling lamb on the corner.

A dingy subway station with parallel customs booths was the dividing line between East and West.

"Maybe you should take that off now—" I said, looking up at Martin's glaringly Western headband. And I wasn't the only one staring at it.

"No, I'm going to keep it on because it stands for peace," he answered defiantly.

"Martin . . . what if a symbol for peace is *mistaken* for a symbol of agitation and starts a conflict? Does it serve its purpose then?"

He didn't have time to answer. I was herded away into the customs line for Americans, of which I was the only one present, and he went through the line with all the other West Germans. I was breezed through with a few sneers and wry smirks, which I took to mean that they were frustrated at not being able to detain me in some way. Then I waited on the Other Side: a darkened baroque station lobby teeming with old people who milled about miserably, waiting to greet relatives from the West. Many of them were crying and a great number of them seemed to be crippled. It was a very sad scene.

I waited and I waited . . . minute upon minute. And then it gripped me—*what had become of Martin?* What were they doing to him? If something really *did* happen, what would I be able to do? I found myself pacing with butterflies in my belly and the look on my face must have approximated the looks of those surrounding me: deathly dread . . . a nameless terror. I was about to ask someone what had happened to him, when out he burst, sans headband, looking ruffled and flushed.

"They searched me—the bastards! Oof! They asked me so many stupid questions—you cannot *believe* it!" I took his arm and we rushed out into the dubious freedom of East Berlin.

"Was it confiscated? The headband?" I asked hopefully.

"Thank God no," he panted, extracting the bunched-up tie from his pants pocket.

"You know, without it, you could pass for Hitler Youth," I laughed, shaking my head.

"I know—and that's what I'm afraid of!" Martin said, tying the white and green band back on his short-cropped blond head.

"Well, I'm glad I wore my cross. We might need it," I sighed, deciding to leave him alone about the headband.

Over here, the first thing I noticed was the cars—the change was immediately apparent. They were all Russian-made, tiny things buzzing around like toys. And the buildings were either very old or very new—there was nothing in between. Huge expanses of cobblestones fanned out before us in all directions. Then we went underground, into a wide, brightly lit tunnel where crowds of people walked.

"I know where we can go: Alexanderstourn! Last time I was here, with my father when I was twelve, I wanted to go up but he wouldn't let me," said Martin.

"Oh, and all this time I thought you were an experienced East-West crosser!" I chided. He was walking faster than I, and this made me aware of a certain phenomenon. The crowds of people passing us in the other direction were turning their heads in unison, like a field of sunflowers in fast motion. I ran to catch up to him, and half-whispered, "Martin, you'd be amazed at the looks you're getting.

Please take it off—I'm afraid." He turned around to meet the glare of the throngs and was visibly nervous. But still he held his ground and refused to take it off.

The Alexanderstourn was very much like the Space Needle in Seattle, with a revolving restaurant on top. Everyone had to wait in regimented lines to go up. There were signs now in German, Polish, and Russian everywhere; I could hear Slavic tongues all around us. While waiting for the elevator, Martin went outside for a smoke and in typical form sat on a railing, which was *verboten*. He had the look of a renegade, and those East German police certainly picked up on it. Instantly he was singled out by two guys in dark blue, who talked into blunt umbrellas—kind of like our plainclothesmen. I was supposed to be waiting inside for the hostess to call our number and I saw all this happening through the glass. Some regular *Polizei* were summoned from around the corner—and PRESTO, Martin was once again being frisked and interrogated, in broad daylight. I came out and beckoned with as sweet and innocent a voice as I could muster, scared though I was, just as they were carting him off.

Perhaps we were just lucky. Or maybe it was his TV press card, or the fact that I was an American. Whatever the reason, he barely escaped an uncertain fate at the hands of the East German police. The incident scared him into finally removing that headband, to my great relief. We went up to the restaurant, where it took a while for Martin to stop shaking. Then for nearly an hour we savored the great variety of marvelous cheap food while gazing at the slowly turning panorama of gray, smogged-in Berlin below.

40

Facing east, over vast unknowable mists of Poland, the subject of Martin's father came up. A heavily decorated general, his father had taken him to a World War II battlefield and proudly showed the heaps of skulls to his seven-year-old son. So it was no wonder that in his little boy's heart the man had always stood for death and hatred. At the age of fifty he had married Martin's mother, then a girl of nineteen, making a tremendous generation gap between them.

After half an hour the revolving restaurant faced west again, and we could see the Wall and some other prominent landmarks poking up out of the haze. Now I began to talk about *my* father: his all-pervasive absence punctuated by the two meetings. As we talked it became clear that we had very different fathers—almost complete opposites. How fittingly ironic that we had each spoken of our fathers in turn, he as we faced east and I as we faced west. It was almost as if our two fathers represented the two hemispheres in some way, his being an Old World soldier and mine a New World writer. And neither of their first languages had been English.

After sampling one of the garishly colored gelatinous desserts the gestapoid waitresses were whisking past our heads (a neon yellow square of sweet rubber with whipped cream on top), we got up and stood on another line, for the elevator down. Martin bumped into some theater friends from Switzerland—it was quite a coincidence to find them here in East Berlin. Here at the very threshold of the free world, where so many Poles, East Germans, and Russians came for a vacation and to get a rare glimpse over the Wall, this cluster of exuberant Western Europeans laughed and embraced and chatted about old times and where they might travel next month, next year . . . Italy, Africa . . . Brazil maybe. I could feel the crowd surrounding us exude the heaviness of solemn envy curdling into contempt. After all, where on Earth could *they* go? Half the world was off-limits to them, unless they excelled in some sport or thought up some ingenious escape plan in a hot air balloon or dug a tunnel. For the first time in my life I felt guilty for having the freedom to travel. Just as one might feel on visiting a friend in prison—when visiting hours are over.

We made one last stop before curfew, a bookstore—once again, the ever-present lineup. Here, separating indoors from outdoors, was a heavy maroon velvet curtain. This oddly appropriate symbol of communism acted as a sort of air lock: ten people were let in as soon as ten people came out.

The concept of browsing, it seemed, was totally unknown here. Everyone grabbed a plastic basket at the door and proceeded to load up on books with single-minded voracity, almost as if they were groceries. These people literally hungered for literature. Even green-coated East German *Polizei* stood in line with impeccable posture, and when their turn came, they took baskets like everyone else. Das Internazionale Buch was huge—it even had a big upstairs. I was amazed at the variety of books and records available, including a great number of American novels with provocative risqué content. Martin asked a clerk if *On The Road* was sold there. She said yes, but that it had been too popular and was therefore discontinued. I bought a little red copy of Karl Marx in Spanish for two DDR marks.

Then back to West Berlin we hurried, through a flurry of dried leaves and chill wind, sharing a box of Mon Cheri cherries with several strangers on the train. Our reentry was such a sharp contrast; it was like walking into a funhouse from a courtroom. This city was an absolute *blast*. Now I understood why freedom felt so exaggerated in West Berlin.

That night and the following day, Martin and I took in a multitude of things, visiting a Picasso sculpture exhibit, shooting pool at some beer joint, holding hands in the mirrored candlelit ambience of the Black Cat Café, then strolling wistfully to the Gedächtniskirche, the Memorial Church—a half-bombed cathedral covered in chicken wire in the middle of a huge place that was like Times Square. Inside there were inscriptions on the wall, written by an American soldier, his last message to the world before he died.

Martin drove me to Hannover on November fifth so that we would have one more day together. Over the bumpy, pothole-ridden highways of East Germany we sped (unlike on the West German autobahn, there was a speed limit of 100 km per hour or about 70 mph). I told him that these roads reminded me of the country roads in the U.S. As the sun was sinking like a giant tangerine into the murky horizon, we were startled by a sudden tremendous roar—it was an old-fashioned iron horse type of locomotive crashing over us on a trestle, spewing thick black plumes of coal smoke. Simultaneously, the vision of two ragged farmers leaning on pitchforks in a field of *blaukraut* arose, the wiggly rows stretching far behind them, not at all perfect and spokelike to drive past like American fields. The sun and the train and the farmers in the field made such a unique picture that I scrambled for my camera, but it was too late.

Perhaps because of that, I recall that vision with crystal clarity over most of the others. It too could have become one in a stack of drab, grainy photos left in a box, but such was not its fate.

In Hannover Martin and I spent our last night together, anxious and overly aware of the passage of time. At dawn we picked some strange little orange lanterns—ground cherries, I think they're called. I kept one as a sort of three-dimensional Valentine memento.

And then, after the immensity of our condensed life in Berlin— three days and four nights spent acutely aware of the falling curtain, the slowly lowering lid over our heads—at last we had to part. On Kleinepfahlstrasse, which means Little Pole Street, we were forced to address the finality of the moment. Having exchanged our little dried orange lanterns and kissed with the weight of heavy molecules, attempting to trick the inevitable half-life of our love, we made the cruel fissure. I walked away. He drove off.

How strange that I could feel so close to him so soon, that I could feel these hot tears of sadness when he leaves, takes his body away— the same caliber as father-desertion tears. And I dare not let him see that I am crying because, after all, this is only four days old, a new affaire. I breathe deeply and pretend to be brave. Time has kept its word. I watch the small car accelerate to the corner carrying the cramped six-foot man. It turns, gone from view.

I wander in the courtyard like a lost weeping waif. There's not much time, they're waiting for me upstairs. But I'm not really here anymore. I too have left. Gone in spirit. All I want to do is sleep and sleep and dream myself back in Berlin with Martin. But *Hamburg* . . . a reading in only three hours!

41

Hamburg . . . another address scrawled on a scrap of paper. Huge ugly city that seems to stretch forever with nightmarish lights like some sort of spaceship landing dock. Army. Things have gone sour.

"*Admiralitätenstrasse fünfundzwanzig, bitte.*" My German pronunciation has improved immeasurably since Berlin, but the cab driver doesn't believe such a place exists. It can't be a true address because it's not in a residential neighborhood. He almost refuses to take me there, but I get pissed and explain that it's a tiny underground bookstore and that I'm expected there ten minutes ago.

Just before the reading, in the yellow glare of the low-ceilinged place in the midst of crowds and confusion there's a telephone call—for *me*. Who? How can this be? Then the hair on the back of my neck bristles with terror when I recognize that voice. It's that man again—the persistent weirdo—*still* after me! I had forgotten all about him. And once again, in keeping with his pattern, he's (thank God) three hundred miles away but desperately wants to come see me even if it means racing at full speed all night to reach Hamburg. How does he find out where I am? I tell him no, I'll be leaving for Frankfurt airport tomorrow and don't have time to see him.

"Why didn't you come to Tübingen?" I ask, hinting that he has missed his chance. Then, in the middle of his frantic raving, I have to hang up on him again. I'm a half hour late to read.

During the reading I stick to childhood parts, feeling that my debauched adult escapades would be too intense for this audience— but even more so, they would be too much for *me* in my present spooked state. There's an odd hostility in the air. Halfway through, some bombs go off down the street. One woman is staring at me with razor-sharp icicles in her eyes. What does she want? I don't feel up to this at all, baring my soul to these cold strangers and stumbling over my own printed words. . . . Help—*Martin!* The question and answer period is even worse. Someone is giving me the third degree:

"Did you like growing up in New York?"

"Well, yes . . . it was all I knew as a child . . ."

"Then Boulder, Colorado, must be awfully boring for you now."

"I wouldn't call it *boring*—different in many ways . . ."

"Your previous life was so full of adventure, and now it must seem so uneventful to lead such a normal stable existence—" He fixes me with a goading stare, his tone provocative in a nasty way. Suddenly the combined events of the whole evening reach a breaking point and anger flares up in me.

"One's life *does* change and, hopefully, evolve, you know. I assure you, Boulder, Colorado, can be quite eventful." The sensation of spitting fire back at this cocky fellow is satisfying, but at the same time I realize that I've let the sharks have a taste of blood. Finally I get a genuinely intrigued question from a young woman— the only nice one of the evening. But on the whole, I'm really fed up and couldn't care less for the belligerent crowd. And they can really sense it, of course. This is the first reading that has been a total failure, out of eight throughout Germany. It must be something in the air . . . the planets perhaps . . . and then it occurs to me—this is the day the sun is transiting my *Mars*. It happens only once a year. Aggression. I am so mad I feel like crying.

Later at the institutional-type building where I am staying in a strange metallic office with an elevated bed near the ceiling, I start my period. Weirdos, anger, fear, Mars, blood. Now it all comes together into a paranoia stew that compels me to put on my cross. Eighteen-carat gold, from the duty-free shop at the Toronto airport. It has served me well so far: it astonished Buddhists at Dorje Dzong in Boulder, helped me blend in with Italians in New York. . . . And now it will protect me from vampires in Hamburg. I take a terrified bath at 2 AM while the phone rings incessantly in the next room. I am sure it's that maniac trying to reach me—but where's he calling from? How did he get the number? Is he spying on me from some nearby warehouse? It seems that whoever it is *knows* I'm here. I climb into the alien bed for a damp, tormented sleep. It is one of those nights on which all one can think of is *the next morning*.

And arrive it did, at long last, revealing a horrific grayness in place of the gruesome blackness of night. Perhaps one day I would return to Hamburg in a more positive light, but this time it was manifested as sheer evil. I hightailed it out of there to the south— got a ride with a girl on her way to Köln with paintings for an art exhibit. Hilde had been up all night finishing them and was very tired, so I wound up driving quite a stretch on the autobahn. And what a rush it was! Merging into the slow lane at 80 mph—so smooth. Once you get going it doesn't feel like you're moving any faster than usual; it's just like being on a stepped-up conveyor belt— UNTIL those demonic headlights flash in the rearview mirror (which has to be checked constantly with darting eyes). Even when there are three miles of visibility in back and not a thing in sight, the next split second a BMW is right smack on your tail like a crazed bat, and your speedometer says 160 kmph (100 mph) . . . and you wonder, *Well, how fast must he be going if he passes me like I'm standing still?*

After a while I managed to get the German-made Ford Escort a tad above 100, just enough to move into fast-lane status. When I'd come up to a slower car and slow down, Hilde would wake up and say, *"Schneller! Schneller!!"* balling up her fist in encouragement and declaring, *"Good* driving," before falling back to sleep. I felt a little like an astronaut, and found, to my surprise, that I had no desire to come down to Earth. Visions of moving to Germany and buying a Porsche danced in my head as the sun set like a sugar plum behind the pale green spires of Köln Cathedral.

My last two days in Europe were spent with Pociao and Roberto, my German translators. They were like an elfin mother and father to me—after the horrors of Hamburg, such a comfort to be with them in Bonn. The three of us traipsed around the capital at a leisurely pace, sliding into sidewalk cafés, inspecting their gardens-to-be under mounds of autumn leaves near the railway tracks, wandering into Bonn's gigantic cathedral in time for evening choir. Cherubic blond Pociao with her curls, a Polish Catholic; Roberto, *un gato* born in Madrid and saturated with Catholicism all through childhood in Brazil; and mongrel me, a heathen from New York, accidentally baptized Catholic as an infant—a motley trio of devotees. We skipped gleefully around on the circular cobblestones, past a corroded block of Roman stone, black and pockmarked by the centuries, one of the first foundations; then inside to see Islamic stained-glass windows. I was in awe over the windows, Roberto was disrespectful of the statues, and Pociao, quiet as a mouse, was seriously pious and peeved at Roberto for his trespasses. At one point we all stood over a grate in the floor, marveling at what seemed to be the smell of grilled hot dogs emanating through it. "Do you think that's Hell down there?" I ventured. All three of us stifled spasms of laughter and left.

That night at their apartment, which they were both anxious to vacate after three years of suppressed creativity, surrounded by old ladies' wallpaper and the deathlike ticking of clocks in the hallway, we sat in loudly squeaking wicker chairs in the kitchen and talked into the wee hours over tea and inspiration. Roberto, strobing the busy wallpaper with his professional flash equipment, took a slew of photos of me wearing various veils.

In bed, I called Martin in Berlin. He had caught a cold, and we said our reluctant final good-byes over the phone through his sniffles and sneezes. He spoke some Portuguese with Roberto, which made me very happy—I had wanted them to meet. Not enough time! I fantasized about being a teenaged German girl in her parents' house, talking to her boyfriend on the phone . . . then reeled into a short sweet sleep. In the morning I felt my throat catching with dryness and realized I couldn't swallow—then I knew. That last night with Martin in Hannover I had caught his cold, then incubated for two days. Knowing where I'd gotten the cold made it all right. Even *nice*. A parting souvenir to nurse.

My two dear friends saw me off on that chill rosy morning at the Hauptbahnhof, right up to the very last moment when I stepped onto the departing train. "See you soon," I lied hopefully, half knowing that "soon" could well become *years*. . . . Still, a drop in the bucket in evolutionary terms.

42

Early in the dawn-dark on a train barreling down the Rhein . . . You're all alone . . . going back home. Everything's done . . . not enough time. You see grapevines stretching almost vertically down steep embankments—some are extra scraggly in the autumnal yellowing of things. Blackened castles peer over cliffs and you strain your neck and eyes to look as you crash by so fast. *Der zug geht* so *schnell* that you are actually afraid to walk through the cars—the furious roar of metal strafes your ears. You haven't learned nearly enough German; two more months and it might have reached a point of entry, like a blotter in your brain soaking up a pool of encroaching India ink . . . black . . . *noir* . . . *negro* . . . *nero* . . . *schwarz*.

You feel you're a coward, running back to the silicon bosom of vast safe America to hide from the immediacy of missiles in comfortable uneventful suburbia, perchance to watch

187

the fireworks of a Euro war on multicolored multicabled radar-dish TV? (Maybe that guy in Hamburg had a point after all.) Are you deserting your newfound friends on this magical, shaky ground where every moment has the true character of being possibly the *last* moment, leaving the land of such tightly compressed cultural fruitcake, these kingdoms of heartfelt debate and long inspired talks over *kaffee und brot*—such close camaraderie and communion when we could all be blown to smithereens by the powers that be.

Something has really changed inside you. Boulder can no longer claim such magic as it did at first. The Flatirons, amazing geological structures though they may be, are just not enough of a reason to cling, lichenlike, to one spot on this poor old globe. Now you are more confused than ever about where to live. Before, the criterion was often *safety*; overnight it has become intriguing *danger*.

Over the shimmering sea, grave of Atlantis, arcing across mammoth mudbanks of time . . . backward and forward at the speed of fright, breaking the ground barrier at a platitude of 30,000 feet. Wings of steel, scratched and streaked by wind-ghosts of the upper atmosphere—bolted securely on, we hope.

Back to the downy bed of Vespucciland you flee now—to what end? You're late, for a very important gate! Away from the missiles, to the home of the missiles—far from the Wall—toward the plains of wasteful freedom. Home of the grave. Purple mountain's majesty, a travesty in mauve. Buddhist in a suit. Pigs in a blanket. Procrastination knocks. Opportunity walks . . . delirium trembles with hope.

November 7. No snow yet. I was surprised to find Denver unburied and clear—easily could have run into a blizzard and a closed airport. Stapleton's vapid yellow halls and whining announcements were a blunt crash landing to reality—I had returned to the biggest hick town in the USofA (with skyscrapers 'n' everything!). And there was

Malcolm in his blue Chevy van, faithfully waiting. We embraced with the recognition of estranged blood kin—nearly a month had elapsed. Much more had transpired than anyone would have dreamed. Life and its ever-present extravagance had kept a promise.

Roaring through "the Mousetrap" on the freeway going toward Boulder, I found that Malcolm's hot-rodding style of driving no longer alarmed me in the slightest. Not after the autobahn. In fact, I had the strongest desire to tell him, "C'mon—faster!" Some aspects of me had unquestionably changed. He looked over at me and could sense the changes. I felt as though I had been on an interstellar journey that had made me younger; and that back home on Earth people were older—older in flesh terms but not in soul growth.

The blue plastic bag with its giant picture of Gauloises was still intact, resting at my feet, and it still contained the German *Kronig Kaffee* and *Schwarzkirsch Konfiture*. All had survived the reentry into the stratosphere all right. I looked forward to the next step—laying out wondrous treasures acquired on foreign turf to wow the folks back home on the range.

But the truth was, I really wanted to keep on going, to spin off into orbit—I hated to stop. I had gathered so much momentum that the idea of coming in for a landing was extremely distasteful. Fever welled up in me like antibodies fighting off the Western Hemisphere, and a pleasant delirium came to the rescue just in time to exempt me from any responsibility. Too much to face. The invalid had returned from strange lands to land in the midst of alien familiarity. My fragile insanity was accepted, and kind souls put me to bed and pulled up the covers. I slipped under the down-filled comforter like an L-1011 slips beneath cloud cover. And that very night the first snow fell, silently as snow does fall. I slipped under the clouds, under the covers, and under the first snowfall. The snow had been patiently awaiting my return. I was very touched by this, and tears began to fall onto the comforter as white blankets fell softly upon the house and the mountains from the silent sky. The kind souls looked in on me and thought I was crying for something or someone else. Who really knows what anyone cries for? *Thank you, snow, for waiting.*

43

Coldest of cold, that winter of '84 in Boulder—below zero for two weeks solid. I went cross-country skiing along the sidewalks downtown, freezing my toes off in January, musing on such things as the overabundance of freedom in the air, the effect of which was similar to lack of oxygen. Here in the States there was so much freedom that nobody knew what to do with it or themselves, whereas in East Berlin the omnipresent oppression had been inspiring. The people there, though solemn, seemed to have an inner fire burning. They were like scuba divers: thirty feet down with lots of pressure per square inch on their bodies; but everything they saw, no matter how tiny, was fabulously beautiful; each thought was appreciated. Or at least that was the impression I got. These were the winged things that flapped across the big screen of my mind on those blander-than-bland afternoons.

Malcolm was always off fixing burst pipes or seeing his current *sangha* woman, Faith, rummaging among his tools like an eternal little boy with very important Tinker Toys. Erector sets—a marvelous collection of metal erections. At this point I knew I was going to leave. The only thing stopping me now was the check-in-the-mail syndrome, which kept me waiting, waiting, waiting. But *this* time when it came I would take the money and *run*, not hang around in this town which was like chewing gum chewed dry of flavor. I didn't even have any anger left. Europe had purged me of anger, and since anger was the main lesson Boulder had taught me, what was left to do here?

I knew that Malcolm could no more help his pattern of pathologically inconveniencing everyone than I could help my own neurotic habits. Within me, a part of me, was the impression made on my little toddler mind when I had held hands with my mother on New York sidewalks, looking up at her strong *I-can-do-it-all-by-myself* beautiful model's face. Surely that was no more intense than the imprint, stamped on little Malcolm's wet concrete heart, of his father in the toolshed in Eugene, pounding and sawing and nailing, his jaw set in determination, forever building things for his family whether they needed them or not.

Perhaps even more telling was Malcolm's vision of his mother standing in the kitchen, always easygoing, so soft that Malcolm knew he could get away with any amount of brattiness: beat up his sister, make his brother eat poisonous flower bulbs, scream and yell so much that she had a nervous breakdown and sent him to live with the preacher. Or my own image of my invisible far-off father, away on wild roads and adventures, becoming famous for all the world but not for me.

Malcolm and I were like two pieces of wood mitred wrong, like mismatched jigsaw puzzle pieces. Malcolm's solution to this was to take the pieces of wood into his father's toolshed and make them fit—*burn* them if necessary. But my solution was my mother's tried-and-true method: to simply *leave*.

Walking along the road, acutely aware of each step, texture of graying blacktop, pebbles crunching, I think of how it is to be ravished by Malcolm. No longer does the idea excite me—rather, now it is repulsive. Why the change? His smooth skin, once so enchanting, I now remember as a revolting smoothness, almost slimy. Touching him is like making love to a giant frog—perhaps because I have so many associations of betrayal and anger and hurt while feeling this skin. I see his sudden toothy grin, flashing like a light bulb for no apparent reason other than some inner self-satisfaction which through conditioning and habit he thinks should be made public. Maybe he believes in some asinine platitude such as "When you smile, the whole world smiles with you." Not necessarily so, bub. Not if you're smiling with evil glee at your torture victim, or smiling smugly at the proud thought of how much chaos you've just managed to create, standing in the middle of it all in fiendish paroxysms of delight, a thirty-three-year-old brat who's driving his family nuts. It's even worse, if you then go meditate at Dorje Dzong and put on your phoney Buddhist smile and nonthink to your cross-legged nonself, "Boy, I sure woke those people up and forced them to address their neuroses!"

Back inside the house, acutely aware of motionless feet having arrived at a destination, I now think of how it was to walk along the road: the cool currents wafting from piney ditches, sunlight needling gentle shafts through branches—the seeming importance of being on one's way somewhere. Why didn't I think of it then, when it was happening? Do things have to marinate in themselves before we are able to appreciate them fully? This strikes me as plausible.

I make cocoa on the blackish stove, in a small chipped enamel saucepan, the blue-and-white spotted sort. Murphy's law besets my solitude and I spill splats of milk and sprinklings of brown powder on the counter. Curse. Why on earth was I thinking of Malcolm on my walk? He must still have a spell on me, a power to infuriate even now. This is disturbing.

Gomer Pyle is much more interesting than the typewriter. I try to fool myself into believing that these silly shows are giving me ideas—theatrical input for screenplays. But the truth is, I'm a TV baby, even though I seldom had a TV as a child, and television makes me feel secure. Ahh yes, the uncanny incongruity of that secure feeling, shared with millions of fellow Americans: the explosive sounds of a war movie in the next room—TV and cocoa—war movie, blanket, and pillow—warm and cozy we fall asleep to the soothing cadence of bombs on the tube.

So—I can be mindlessly secure if I want to, Goddamnit! Who's gonna stop me, huh? The rebellious teenager in me lashes out— but there's no one here to rebel against. My self is infinitely understanding. In recent years the world has managed to instill (or install) a new feeling in me: guilt. It's like a gramophone introduced to Borneo tribesmen in the twenties.

44

Juarez, February 7 . . . Malcolm's birthday. My *compañero* and I had walked across the hellish border bridges three times, back and forth in the limbo between El Paso and Mexico. The problem was that Malcolm hadn't brought a passport, only his driver's license. So in order to procure a tourist card for him, we had to run all over El Paso to find a notary public who could witness me vouch for his citizenship. Otherwise the Mexicans wouldn't let us in. But when we were about to get on the train for Chihuahua there was yet another inscrutable mix-up, a missing signature or some such rot. All the insanity of Mexican bureaucracy came slithering back like a vat of eels into my memory: the fiasco in 1967 with John . . . *federales* trooping into our A-frame hut at night in Yelapa when I was fifteen and pregnant. . . .

I took all this as an omen that we should just scrap Mexico and get down to Florida or some Gulf Coast place, but Malcolm pushed stubbornly through and bribed the railway officials. So there we were, merrily clacking our way south on the *ferrocarril*, a blackened nightmare train which said PRIMER CLASE ESPECIAL on the outside—the very same kind of train that John had carried me onto when I couldn't walk after the baby had been stillborn in the Yelapan jungle and all the Mexican guys were looking up my dress because John couldn't catch the hem of it under his arm as he hassled with tickets and luggage—and I had hidden my face in his shoulder, pretending not to exist at all. . . .

But this was all brand new to Malcolm. Bright-eyed, he squirmed around in his seat like a kid at a Disney World. Having drunk several strong Mexican beers, he began toying with Spanish words, loudly, in an atrocious American accent. Once again I found myself wanting to hide my face—but not in Malcolm's shoulder.

A crooning, wailing Mexican song seeped into our car from some small radio as the driest of deserts sped by, and suddenly I was stricken by an ultimate sadness for this man beside me, asleep now. How awful that I had reached the end of my rope with him *now*—on his *birthday*—the day we had both spoken of so hopefully: "Well, we should be basking on a sunny beach by your birthday!"

But I had absolutely nothing left to say to him anymore. And the trip was just beginning. I felt like a duplicate key that, with a great display of sparks and high-pitched whining of brass, had been filed to match his and was now just sitting there in the whirring vice grip—ready to be polished and set free. At this dismal dark tail end for me, which in a sense was only the beginning for him, I wondered with a shudder what might come next.

SAAANWEEEECHES!

A little man was squeezing through the narrow aisles of the train with a pailful of sandwiches: the most generic and boring type imaginable, white bread and bologna with mayonnaise. I bought two, realizing that heaven had sent me a distraction. At least shelter, sleep, and food could always be relied upon for avoidance of an issue.

Malcolm woke up and ate his sandwich.

"Hey—mine has a hot green chile in the middle!"

"Really? Oh, so does mine. Wow, that's *good*."

The mere discovery of these chiles, one to each sandwich, hidden between the deceptively insipid slabs of Wonder bread, was so surprising that I forgot all about having nothing left to say. We bought some beers too, from another guy with a pail, and more and more of the amazing *saaanweeches*, and wound up having a great discussion about very simple things as we hurtled like lost meteorites through the Mexican night.

Then came the strange blue ice-cream shop in Chihuahua, and our crazy plunge through the Copper Canyon, during which time the train came to a screeching halt seven times and Malcolm explained to some terrified Americans that the brakes of a train came on automatically whenever the pressure hose broke. Out of the high cold desert now, I began to see baby palms nestled in rock gorges— enthralling signs of the tropics drawing near. Hanging out the side between cars in the quickly warming night air, I caught heady fragrances of tropical blossoms mysteriously zooming by, down, down, down. The inexorable plunge toward the Sea of Cortez felt terrific. And I was sorry I had been so hard on Malcolm.

Los Mochis, with its crazy filthy tropical city chaos and ludicrous view of the splashing turquoise fountain splashing right in front of the hideous black spewing smokestacks of the *azucadero* sugarcane plant, was so incongruous that it made us laugh together, and Malcolm and I made love again in the strangeness of a half-demolished hotel room for old times' sake, reconstructing a certain poignancy— painting yet another layer of illusory lacquer over the many-coated walls of our hearts.

On the ferry to La Paz he sheltered me from the wind on the upper deck and talked with the English-speaking captain about the workings of the ship, reminding me how admirable was his knowledge of things mechanical. The romance of the boat infected us, and we allowed it to because we preferred to be lovers in love on a boat instead of lovers breaking up on a boat. There would be time for that later. Elsewhere.

45

The very tip of Baja, between crashing Pacific and placid Mar de Cortez, became the elsewhere we needed. In Cabo San Lucas, at the Hotel Marina, Malcolm and I broke up with great flamboyance. One evening when I was feeling a bit feverish after a whole day in the sun, Malcolm pinned me down on the bed, me under the covers and he on top, and proceeded to lecture me on Buddhist dogma— and accused me of being negative. I felt so frustrated, pinned under all the bedding, so furious to be put in such a position, that a volcano welled up inside me as he lectured in his soft-sell Jehovah's Witness voice.

All at once my anger erupted underneath him and somehow with a scream of rage I flung him off me, blankets and all, and attacked him like a wildcat—

I stopped when I realized I had actually made a gash in the flesh of his sunburned arm. Never before had I been pushed to such limits of violence. He went off to the beach without me that day, and later, when we had each had time to cool down, he brought back someone he had met on La Playa del Amor.

The savage fury and hatred I felt for Malcolm, enacted in our wretched hotel-room fights behind flimsy shutters and overheard by clusters of tiny immature mangoes, was blessedly neutralized by the Israeli. Adi became our unwitting referee to such an extent that Malcolm and I no longer even focused on each other. This presence which came between us now was a long-awaited eclipse. His voice—deep, soothing, chortly, and redolent of Middle Eastern white cliffs, olive trees, biblical deserts—was hypnotic. And through his thick accent shone a brilliance, a refreshing genius to play with. We played with him in different ways, each refracting a different facet at the same time, and as a result all three of us had a ball, whether on the beaches we'd discovered, on the dusty streets of Cabo, or in thatched restaurants by night.

I was no longer the sole translator of Spanish for Malcolm. Our new companion, besides reinforcing the Spanish I knew, delighted in making cross-lingual puns in Hebrew, English, and French, and could make even the glummest of Mexican waiters laugh uproariously.

After this strange end-of-the-line limbo on the tip of rock-studded Baja, an incident with retarded police over my stolen cross, the invasion of potbellied ex-marines on our beautiful beach, we set off for a different dimension altogether—a dream of another color.

Todos Santos (irreverently rechristened Ningunos Santos by Adi) was just the place to find ourselves on Saint Patrick's Day. We stumbled upon a palatial guest house, complete with diaphanous mosquito netting over all the beds, a vine blooming with *copas de oro*—cups of gold—draped around the patio, baroque foyer and dining room so oddly out of place in these semi-arid coastal tropics. It was like a Luis Buñuel film.

The magic words "Caspar sent us" got us into this through-the-looking-glass place. And to top it off, the very next day after we arrived, the owners went away, leaving us all alone in the place to take care of it while they were gone! We were landlords for a day and could rent the rooms out to anyone as we saw fit.

Strolling down the long road to the beach, we ran into a tanned Canadian couple with decidedly dilated pupils who looked quite lost, a doctor and his buxom wife, fresh from Esalen. The three of us took the two of them under our wing, and we all spent a day on the beach together. . . .

This beach, unlike the one at Cabo, is far away through stretches of palms and cactus fields. So the five of us take a taxi out to where the waves are curling in. Walking toward the water, I am reminded of the movie *The Four Hundred Blows*.

At first we all sit on a big yellow towel and talk. The doctor and his wife dole out some Orange Sunshine. God! I suddenly realize that I haven't taken LSD since 1970—*fourteen years!* But I accept a smallish crumb. It seems appropriate.

Even before the spirit of ergot has a chance to wisp through my bloodstream, I think I know what will happen: observing these five people, myself included, I see the quintessence of character in each one. Malcolm will throw himself at the sea, Adi will talk to himself and impersonate Gary Larson cartoons, I will toy with my turquoise shroud and make it billow in the breeze, imagining myself to be some sort of Egyptian scribe, the doctor will struggle hilariously with his drawstring pants while trying to smoke a cigar, and Leslie will writhe sumptuously in the sand.

The day roars on, waves approaching endlessly as if on a huge conveyor belt. Malcolm is way out there, his barrel-chested self embracing the water. I wonder if he will disappear into the sea. My simple prophecy is bearing itself out as, in turquoise veil, I slash rapturously at the beige upper layer of sand with a long stick, down through to black sand beneath to scribble these glyphs which feel so right: "Coca Cola" in Arabic. And then in Hebrew, which Adi shows me. The beach is now strewn with Egyptian eyes and ankhs and the number five, all dating back to early acid trips with Paul. I am Lawrence of Arabia, or some anonymous Babylonian—an eternal kid playing in an enormous sandbox on purpose. Adi keeps strolling absently by, admiring my work and speaking in different languages. Leslie and Michael are running around in circles, chasing each other's tails. She falls in the sand and he struggles with his drawstrings. What an unusual day!

Then, like cave dwellers, we all become gradually aware of a monstrous shift, a minor catastrophe in our little warm-blooded lives—

THE SUN IS SETTING

We huddle wordlessly on the towel once again. Malcolm is the last to notice this phenomenon, because he's been more active than the rest of us. Our shivering gives birth to a new preoccupation with fabric: towels, clothes. The doctor is even more hilarious now, with his tangled shirts and scarves. We all begin to laugh uncontrollably with shuddering taffy spasms in our jawbones. I turn away from the sea and face a sun-warmed stand of palms, walk over and embrace their dry, crackly trunks.

Someone has a bright idea and builds a fire. It's all so basic, so predictable, so perfectly human. Adi and I have some wondrous telepathy going about the sticks—they're HARD. Almost as hard as stones, but not quite. We grin at each other over the flames, flashing our Cro-Magnonesque teeth while deliriously fondling the pieces of driftwood, pressing them into the sand with our heels, and pushing our flesh-padded skeletons against each other. We are in love with things solid.

It's dark. A full moon comes up over palms and cacti and Leslie says, "I wonder what time it is." We all remember at once, as we stare into the writhing demons of fire, that we had arranged for a taxi to pick us up at 7 PM—but no one has a watch. Leslie jokingly stands up on the deserted beach and waves her hand as if she's in midtown Manhattan: "Taxi!" And out of nowhere, magically, the Mexican taxi appears. It's too much of a coincidence.

We're all laughing crazily, also remembering what palatial quarters await us, as we squeeze together in the cab like a boxful of unpitted dates and rumble back to Todos Santos through enchanted yuccas and saguaros glowing in the blue-white moonlight.

46

The Sangre de Cristo range slept soundly, mountainously secure in its rocky selfhood. No tremors or upheavals had disturbed its dreams for centuries, though there were many stone necklaces draped high and dry around the necks of old ponds, reminding the earth of ancient waterlines which even the ponds had forgotten by now. Piñon trees stretched and yawned in the mauve predawn and ever-vigilant clouds did slow-motion acrobatics for the *chamisa* bushes, making them blush and bow their heads toward the dry *arroyos*. But the land itself slept like a rock. Unseen jackrabbits skirted the yucca on supernatural stilts, and red ants narcissistically collected pinkish bits of granite to mirror their own roseate armor.

As the crow swoops, high and low from the wheatfields of eastern New Mexico, soaring and dipping over peaks named Blood of Christ (though he never has cared what the humans called his mountains), he sees every detail below, near and far, including the sudden crescent of earth-cubes which humans call *adobe*.

Going west in the 9,000-foot crystalline breath of April, in one of the first of these dwellings he sees three creatures reside, snugly unaware of themselves on that morning. Two humans and a feline float in blankets and fur inside the shelter of crumbling rock, rotting beams, and plinking radiators which is rooted firmly in the hillside above Palace Avenue, overlooking Santa Fe. . . .

Bare feet on gritty flagstone . . . half awake I enter the studio, John's back porch, recently roofed in with plastic: enormous terrastrology wheels, blackboard, and potbellied stove. Baby elms grow out of the floor. . . .

A dream come true. I'm really here—not in Boulder anymore, or Baja. Malcolm is *gone*. I'm free at last. Free to be myself and enjoy a cradled hermitage with my best and oldest friend.

The headiness of the air, the crinkly crunch of leaves outside, distinctive rough wooden poles leaning against the window—it's all a new life. New senses. A new nose, new eyes, new ears. How fortunate to have so many lives within one life. I startle myself: who's that woman in the mirror? Sun-bleached hair, Mexican tan, wearing John's big black kimono . . . I don't recognize her.

Writing on the blackboard with pink chalk is most gratifying. It's like being back in elementary school again. I tighten the sash on the kimono and bound down three steep steps to the kitchen. The blackened gas range is fabulously strange to behold in its trusty oldness, like New York. Dutch coffee in a vacuum pack is like something I discover as a toddler doing mischief in the house before my mother wakes up. I cut the gold paper and PLOOF it sighs, loses its brick shape and becomes aromatic all at once—like magic. I am a cave woman: inventing fire, touching a cat, discovering my feet, all for the first time.

Ahh . . . John is waking—smells the coffee, hears my clatter.

It's Christmas morning in April and all of life is a present left under the tree.

What is it that makes me shudder so? It's a specter, a specter of Malcolm. He's giggling mischievously, his little-boy-turned-man face ashen with pallor from asthma. He's getting down on his hands and knees with his toolbox. Those meddlesome hands all rough and coated with metallic dirt, grease, and chemicals are coming to fix me like a sink. He's crawling under me now, between my legs with wrenches, snakes, plungers, butane torches. He's gleefully bollixing up my inner sanctum with his plumber's know-how. I kick at him wildly, trying to smash his head, but—horror of horrors—he's an indestructible doll of some sort! He coaxes, "Aw, c'mon," smiling like the Pillsbury doughboy, head cocked to one side in false bashfulness, eyes glassy, thinking only of his tools, his TOYS! I'm paralyzed here in the clutches of the Fixit Man—welded to a porcelain bowl—in the Toilet Zone!

Water running deep . . . a profound pummeling sound shakes me from the vice grip of the awful dream— A high stucco ceiling—John's house. *Relief.* It's only John running his ginger bath. What's expected of me here? Not a thing. No rules at all. I can wake up at 5 PM or 2 AM. Gone are the dreadful obligations of a love affaire gone bad. What I have with John is a love of sheer power—crystalline flower—timeless as it should be. I step out under the April sky, crunching pebbles under bare feet, and thank the lords for my will. Have I died and been issued a new body so soon? John loves me and I love him, but it's like stone. Needs no explanation. I am so lucky. . . . He takes his bath and doesn't need me to watch, doesn't care what I'm up to. He types rapidly like an insect in the other room, and doesn't call to me. I lounge on the crumbling balcony, listening to Brazilian music in the sun . . .

stroll on the roof . . . plant lentils in the tiny rock-ledge garden. We are like Papillon and Degas on Devil's Island, two old coots co-existing in timeless harmony, waiting for the big plunge, the long drift.

47

So now after all this, the true flavor comes through . . . You thought it would be bitter but it's only nutty after all. The cup at your teeth chatters in triumph. Like a knave caught with his pants down in a stable, *men* are finally clarified for you: little boys grown up. Innocents and psychos alike take on a new softness. A pane of glass between you and the world has been sprayed clean, though you know it will soon collect another film of dustlets. The black man in a suit, carrying a shotgun, his own little boy buried far within, sinks down into straw, preparing for a long journey. A chorus of women's voices grates from the radio—"Freeeeeeeee"—like several different kinds of vinegar.

Outside later, while trudging past dried-up adobes, a burnt smell will come to your nostrils, all the way from New York City and your childhood, a smell which was no doubt created by some men burning trash or perhaps pretzels. Men are all about—manly men, glorious men, running the world as they have indeed always done. But no man is in your bed—at the moment. What is the meaning of this masculine vacuum? Is God conducting an experiment? Men are out there being adventurous, filling the stories you've heard: wondrous tales of storms at sea, restaurant heists, smoky sixties scenes from Minton's Playhouse in Harlem. These are the myths of your girlhood, these realms of intensely dangerous glamour, glorified crime, far-off lands, inaccessible even to most men.

So is it really any wonder that you choose the paths seldom taken? It was all in the cards, the house of cards, the condemned tenements of cards in which you grew up. And now, now that all has fluttered down to the ground, upset by the swinging pendulum of a wrecking ball which may be only the brass counterweight of a grandfather clock, now that all the bricks and lathe and plaster and cards have fallen and burned along with the trash and pretzels, now that the ash has blown away, you can finally see. The smoke has cleared and there is room now for other dreams. Ashes to ashes, dusk to dusk.

And the perennial "I love you"—so taboo that we feel compelled to try it out anyway, as a sort of exorcism to prove it doesn't matter even though it does. The eyes—*watch the eyes*. To stare unwaveringly into the eyes of the other . . . there's the rub. Blue eyes looking at green eyes beholding azure eyes staring into hazel eyes piercing gray eyes bathing emerald eyes streaming through sapphire eyes adoring onyx eyes . . . and something magic takes place. The whole face begins to shimmer with life force, sheer animal power . . . a feeling of fusion—twin fetuses in cellular bondage. Sweat, heat, tears. . . . oh so old, so well known, yet the mystery never ends, forever reborn. Flesh and blood tipping the scales of a giant golden carp.

I'm stuck fast, a South Carolina tar-baby in this ancient Chinese tapestry. With a golden needle quivering in my left ankle and a silver one in my right wrist, I lie in the realm of water dragons, utterly calm, watching blue smoke spiral up from my feet as the warm horseshoe of a meridian comes to life.

Don't fondle the doctor. Br'er Terrapin has fallen on his back an' can't get up. Lord, Lord, Lord, you don't know what trouble is till you fall on your back an' can't get up. By 'n by Br'er Rabbit come an' help you outta dat hole. But what if de doctor wear shorts, an' your hand jes' touch his balls? Br'er Fox can't *help* but fondle de doctor *den*. So shame on the shaman. Daddy don't live in dat New York City no more . . . Daddy don't live nowhere, no more.

And so time passes, passes by, passes over, passes away and through and pass the butter, please. Sometimes time passes by so fast . . . you can't even see those seconds make their little streaks of reentry into your heart.

Afterword
by Gerald Nicosia

I recall Jan Kerouac talking about her plan to write other books even before she'd finished *Baby Driver*. But a rift began to form between us not long after that first novel was published in 1981, so I was not nearly as close to her during the composition of *Trainsong* as I was during the *Baby Driver* years, when I sometimes got daily progress reports. In many ways, what happened between us was probably inevitable. I had been a mentor for her, and at some point, every original artist needs to reject his mentors. But there was something else going on, a very big something in her life, and in many ways that something became the subject of *Trainsong*. In publishing *Baby Driver*, Jan had stepped across a personal Rubicon, transforming herself from anonymous delinquent and petty criminal into a respectable American literary artist and public personality. And for her, *Jan Kerouac*, that transformation held more perils than for most. It thrust her into the same blinding spotlight of celebrity, with its attendant attention and reverence, that had been focused on her father, whom she had always feared she could never live up to.

In July 1982, the Naropa Institute in Boulder, Colorado, hosted a major ten-day conference to celebrate the twenty-fifth anniversary of the publication of Jack Kerouac's *On the Road*. Allen Ginsberg, chairman of the conference, had come to me for Jan's address, since she had all but disappeared from public view. She was living next door to her mom in a little shantytown area of Eugene, Oregon—a neighborhood right next to the railroad switching yards known as Trainsong Park. Jan and I had even made tentative plans to drive from Eugene to Boulder together. But I had gotten stuck in Chicago that summer—no money and serious health problems—and in the meantime, Ginsberg had sent Jan airfare to Denver. Still, I expected Jan and I would have a warm reunion there.

Instead, she accosted me hostilely in one of the University of Colorado buildings (Naropa had no campus of its own) and accused me of having made people think she was a janitor! After a few dazed seconds, I realized I had simply recounted an episode from one of her recent letters, which described how she had had to clean up a huge mess of broken eggs at the Excelsior Café in Eugene, where she then worked. This was a new Jan: the star worried about her public image. She was suddenly, as Anne Waldman dubbed her, "the Kerouac princess," and it seemed like every nongay man under seventy was making a play to get into her pants. She was literally moving faster than I had ever seen her, dashing out of conversations in mid-sentence and dealing out rude snubs that left not a few mouths gaping. She had taken her place among the famous—"I had fallen into the lap of John Steinbeck, Jr., and cameras had flashed like deranged lightning bugs," she writes in *Trainsong*—and, by taking off all her clothes for romps in the hot tub at various private parties, she wasn't exactly discouraging the attention.

But Jan also performed with dignity on a couple of the panels, reading from both her own work and the still-unfinished memoir of her mother, Joan, *Nobody's Wife*. And though she soon moved in with a prominent young member of the Buddhist community, she worked steadily on her new book during her three years in Boulder, making it clear she was nobody's bimbo but, rather, as serious about her literary profession as all the other ambitious local wordsmiths who aspired to grow out from under Ginsberg's shadow. Allen's encouragement meant a lot to her during those years; and they even had a little Buddhist ceremony there in 1983 in which he officially became her godfather. She also got herself a literary agent in Boulder, Peter Livingston (Milo Trump in *Trainsong*); and through Livingston's help, *Baby Driver* came out in a Holt, Rinehart mass paperback edition, which she promoted in both the United States and Europe. She was, in fact, one of the feature attractions at the One World Poetry Festival in Amsterdam in 1983. That tour, and her meeting with novelist Richard Brautigan in Amsterdam, provided material for one of the most powerful sections of *Trainsong*.

By July 1985, big changes were again happening in Jan's life. She had broken up with her Buddhist lover Michael, had permanently left Boulder, had been given a contract for her second novel by Holt, and was on her way back to her mother's in Eugene. It was also the time for us to renew our friendship. She had been traveling up from Baja California with a new Israeli friend named Adi Gorel (the Adi of *Trainsong*), and while she rested a few days at Adi's home in Palo Alto, she called me for a rendezvous in San Francisco.

I liked what I saw and heard. Jan seemed so much stronger, so much more mature than I had ever known her. She had, for one thing, a far more detached—and, I thought, far healthier—perspective on her mother. Her mother had had a radical mastectomy, which was apparently successful, but she was experiencing problems with her immune system—specifically, a foot infection that wouldn't heal—and Jan planned to nurse her back to health. But she did not plan to live again with her mother. Her mother was "caught in a rut of invalidism and failure and poverty," she told me. Joan had "made a whole life out of saving money, living as cheaply as possible." It angered Jan, for instance, that when she'd take her mother out to a fancy restaurant Joan would get all nervous and upset and tell Jan, "We could've prepared this meal at home for fifty-eight cents." Jan had started making decent money—$7,000 had just come in for English rights to *Baby Driver*, and she'd gotten an $8,500 advance on the new book from Holt—and she was about to get a lot more, because her lawyers had finally concluded an agreement with the family of her father's widow, Stella Sampas, which affirmed Jan's right to collect half of the royalties on several of her father's books beginning in January 1986.

Jan wanted the good life for herself, wanted some leisure to develop talents besides writing, wanted to dabble at being a photojournalist, an actress, and a film-script writer, among other things. But writing was still very much on her mind, and before she quit altogether, she wanted to complete a book she'd already sketched out: a story of five of her reincarnations over the past two thousand years. But it was the new book for Holt, of course, that I most wanted to hear about. She told me she preferred the title "Loverbs," especially since her mother had wanted to use "Trainsong" for a second book she was writing. "Loverbs" would explore the nature of "serial relationships" in modern life, which Jan wanted to rechristen "relays." The pun in "Loverbs" had something to do with her notion that a lover was only interesting and useful so long as he brought some new action into her life; and once each man's particular form of action had ceased to engage her, it was time to move on. She told me her editor at Holt had encouraged her to structure the book as "a diary of all her relationships with men" over the past ten years, and she liked the idea, she said, because it would allow her to play a "goofy, zany character" during the next round of book promotions, rather than make serious pronouncements about her father, as she'd been requested to do on the tours for *Baby Driver*.

I wondered, in view of the fact that she talked of having just taken magic mushrooms again and of having bought and then thrown away a handgun "to keep from doing something drastic with it," whether this talk of serial relationships bespoke some new binge of self-destructiveness. But she assured me that she had actually become "optimistic," that she was learning about "the power of positive thinking," and that she now believed a good relationship was possible if she simply willed herself to move toward it instead of always "backing away." She told me that for years she had been filled with anger at her father for rejecting her but that she couldn't acknowledge it, so she kept seeking men who reminded her of her father to act out that futile drama over and over again. This self-flagellation had reached a peak at the Kerouac Conference in Boulder, she said, when she had to confront thousands of people showing adoration for a man, her father, who had showed no feeling for her whatsoever.

Unfortunately, Jan's optimism and resolve did not spell out a wonderful new life for her. The weight of old patterns quickly reasserted itself; and over the next two years, as she continued to revise and expand the manuscript of what became *Trainsong*, her life grew ever darker and more desperate. While the novel was being printed, in late December 1987, its author just nearly missed being killed. After completing the manuscript, in October, she had gone to Hawaii, ostensibly to realize her "big dream" of having a house in the tropics, close to warm ocean water, where she could snorkel every day, with a garden that would "really tie her down." Instead, shortly after her arrival, she had begun an affair with a married short-order cook named Michael, whom she referred to as "a raging alcoholic Piscean, who was the quintessence of my father." One night, both of them drunk on Jack Daniels and high on a combination of Xanax, Valium, and acid, he smashed a window in his wife's house and stole her Jeep, and he and Jan raced wildly around Maui dodging police cars, with Pink Floyd's *Dark Side of the Moon* blaring from the tape deck. At one point, the two of them had the Jeep hidden under some shrubbery as police searchlights crawled over them. Later, Michael crashed into a tourist's car and kept right on going. Before morning, Jan was in a local hospital having her head stitched up, though she never did say exactly what had happened to her.

She did tell me, however, that she had realized how insane her life had gotten, how stupid it would have been for her to die just as her second book was coming out. She flew back to the continental United States, back to her mother in Eugene again, and immediately started seeing a psychotherapist. On her book tour that spring (1988), she often spoke of her determination to come to grips with her "father complex," admitting that during her youth and twenties she "couldn't see the forest for the trees" as far as the devastating impact of his absence went. She had been misled by the Jack Kerouac legend into thinking her father was larger than life, she explained, which had only made *her* seem small and inessential. She wanted simply to "accept him as a person, as he was," so that she could find some sort of ordinary place in life for herself.

I thought Jan was truly onto something useful, and I was even more impressed when I read *Trainsong*. Her first novel had recounted a teenage girl's remarkable picaresque odyssey across the depths of the 1960s counterculture, as vividly as anything to date, but it had been flawed by the narrator's narcissism and solipsism. One sometimes had the feeling that Jan had turned to literature to mask, rather than reveal, the horrors and degradations of her life. But *Trainsong* reversed all that. Finally, we saw a Jan who broke down, who cried, and, perhaps most revealingly, who got angry at the people who had hurt her. At the end of chapter 32 was a passage that conjured up some of the most powerful emotion I had experienced in contemporary writing:

> Something like a monkey wrench twists in my isolated psyche . . . a baby girl in Albany, New York, says "Mommy" for the first time. And a thirty-year-old woman in Boulder, Colorado, says "Daddy" for the first time in her life . . . whispers *daddy*—toys with the novel syllables . . . screams DADDY. . . . The word reaches into her throat like a rebel with claws, tearing up her soul—my soul, strangling flesh of his flesh—blood of his blood my blood—screaming in the black mountain silence of Bluff Street revisited visitation.

In the review I wrote of *Trainsong* for the *Chicago Tribune* (which never ran), I singled out that passage as the very core of the book. If she continued to write like that, I speculated, she might "someday explore father–daughter relations as thoroughly as Hemingway explored fathers and sons." I was almost as strongly affected by her portrait of Richard Brautigan a year before his suicide. Her empathy with this lost, depressed, alcoholic gentle giant and literary genius seemed to lead her to the verge of admitting as great a sadness and loneliness within herself. If she could ever step through that door, I thought, ever confess the hugeness of her own pain, her writing would be at the forefront of contemporary American fiction.

AFTERWORD

I saw Jan that June in Lowell, Massachusetts, at the dedication of
the outdoor granite sculpture honoring her father. In fact, I had had
a lot to do with bringing her there, since the Sampas family, who
were running the show, had refused to invite her. My friend Brad
Parker, who ran his own independent Corporation for the Humanities in Lowell, had paid her bus fare from Oregon, and my other
Lowell friend, Father Armand "Spike" Morissette, Kerouac's boyhood
priest, had paid for her room at the Lowell Hilton. Still, the Sampases
did not permit her to speak, or even introduce her, at the official ceremony, and she had to sit along with the rest of us on the wet, newly
laid sod beneath the speakers' platform.

There was good reason for her to be glum after such ill-treatment
at an event that supposedly celebrated her father's bighearted hu-
manity, but I knew there was a lot more going wrong with Jan besides
the boorish behavior of her Greek stepfamily. She said her mother
was dying but refused to give me details, putting up the sort of wall
we never before had had between us. She also told me her own legs
had been swelling recently but again declined to elaborate on her
own medical situation. In many ways, I felt as if it were some kind of
replay of 1982 but with an even more tragic edge. She was running
up a huge room-service bill, mercilessly exploiting Father Spike's
and Brad's financial goodwill, and insulting people like Edie Parker
and Henri Cru (her father's first wife and lifelong buddy, respec-
tively) for no good reason. In an ugly scene at Jack Kerouac's grave,
Edie's boyfriend, Tim, told Jan she was disgracing the Kerouac name,
that she couldn't "keep shitting on people and walking away," and
that if she were Jan Smith people wouldn't take such abusive behavior from her.

The truth was that Jan was once again turning her real anger
against herself. Back in Eugene, she plunged into two of the most de-
structive relationships of her life—one with a drunken Irish philan-
derer named Glen, whom she called "The King of Darts," and the
other with a slobbish, parasitic cabdriver she called "Spider." After her

217

mother died on Mother's Day, 1990, she turned to the ultimate form of degradation, working as a stripper in a cheap bar. Then she fell seriously ill, couldn't pay her hospital bill, and fled to Puerto Rico with the intention of faking her own death to escape her creditors. There she hooked up with yet another callous gigolo, who complained of having to drive her to the hospital the night she almost died of kidney failure, in August 1991.

Jan had begun work on what was to have been her final autobiographical novel, "Parrot Fever," even before *Trainsong* hit the bookstores. She wanted to try out writing in the third person and splitting her personality into two sisters, the hardworking writer and the crazy "bad girl," in order to make some final sense of her schizophrenic life. The novel had great promise, but she never lived to finish it. For almost the last five years of her life, she had to do self-dialysis four times a day, every six hours, to stay alive. It was an exhausting process that kept her from ever getting a full night's sleep. Her eyesight was failing badly, so that in the end she could only work on tape. And then there was the lawsuit, which is a whole other story in itself: Jan's drawn-out legal battle with the Sampas family to recover her father's literary archive and preserve it, as he had wished, in some university library or museum.

Still, enough of "Parrot Fever" exists for readers—once it is assembled—to see what she intended: nothing less than a trilogy chronicling the life and death of a Beat icon's child, as complete a portrait as she could make of the legacy bequeathed by these countercultural heroes to her generation. There was a grand acceptance developing in Jan at the very end—a willingness to continue rejoicing in the freedom the Beats, and Jack in particular, had given her, while at the same time acknowledging the inevitable hurt that went along with it. Which is just another way of saying she had learned to love and hate her father at the same time. That she didn't live to spell that out for us in her inimitable style is a shame, but she left us enough to read it between the lines.

The following two interviews with Jan Kerouac, conducted seventeen years apart, show a great deal about her growth as a human being, even as her health seriously declined. The first interview, which I did with Jan in October 1979, when she was in San Francisco to find a publisher for her novel *Baby Driver*, reveals a bright but often self-centered young woman. At that time, Jan alternated between glorying in the attention generated by her celebrity father and struggling to know who her father really was. The second interview, conducted by actress Dianne Jones for an Italian film company in May 1996, a month before Jan's death, shows a far more serious, middle-aged woman confronting her own mortality. The Jan of that last interview has discovered her father's identity by searching herself and by creating a connection between them in her efforts to preserve her father's legacy. Jan's ex-husband John Lash observed wisely that her father had permanently wounded her by denying her his love. He had forced her to find the only route of healing available, which was to offer love and acceptance to the one who had rejected her—to repay cruelty with kindness. There is still anger in that last interview, but it is tempered with a great deal of compassion and human understanding.

I have chosen to reprint the first interview just as I wrote it for *Oui* magazine, which rejected it. It includes some material about Jack Kerouac from our earlier interviews, as well as a short introduction that gives the feeling—the excitement of horizons opening—and also the perpetual goofing and silliness of her visit to San Francisco.

Gerald Nicosia met Jan Kerouac in 1978 when he had just begun researching his biography of Jack Kerouac, *Memory Babe*, recently called by the *Washington Post* "the best of the Kerouac biographies." Nicosia has published hundreds of articles and stories about the Beat Generation and its writers, as well as his own poetry and fiction. For the past ten years he has devoted himself—through more than 500 interviews nationwide—to chronicling the healing process of Vietnam veterans in a forthcoming book called *Home to War: A History of the Vietnam Veterans' Movement*.

A Conversation with Jan Kerouac
October 1979
by Gerald Nicosia

As Jack Kerouac denied that the hippies were the children of beatness, so he also refused to recognize his own daughter, Jan. He didn't pay even a part of her support till after he was taken to court by her mother, Jack's second wife, Joan Haverty, when Jan was ten. Today, at twenty-seven, Jan has written a novel herself, "Everthreads," a tale of hard times that would make the Great Depression sound like a chapter by Erica Jong. Jan's novel grew out of a lifelong search for her father. Raised in the slums of New York's Lower East Side, she survived by robbing the poor box and working as a teenage hooker.[1] At twelve she dropped acid; at thirteen she was shooting methedrine and heroin. After Bellevue, a stillborn baby in the Mexican jungle, two marriages, a gamut of grubby jobs, from dishwasher to racetrack groom, and ceaseless wanderings through North and South America, North Africa, and Europe, she is still taunted by her father's elusive ghost.

Now that the kids Kerouac turned on are becoming the Establishment themselves, she hears his name everywhere on the lips of strangers. Even if her father was a beacon for millions, "Oh, you're Jack Kerouac's daughter!" is definitely not her favorite opening line.

We met for the interview after a celebration at the Old Spaghetti Factory in North Beach on the tenth anniversary of Jack's final "liberation." Jan had spent the party getting drunk, making faces at TV cameras, and trying in a friendly way to set fire to wheelchair vet Ron Kovic.

GN: You're forced to share your father whether you want to or not.

JK: I've had several run-ins with intellectuals who were crazy

---

[1] Jan later told me that her hooking was quite brief; mostly she survived by living with her mother, who was on welfare, and at state expense while she was detained in a variety of youth homes.

about my father. One guy was a complete parasite. He kept asking me about Kerouac, as if that's all he lived for. I'm rather hard on people like that, who don't have any self-dignity. It has something to do with the ego of not wanting to be the daughter of someone famous. Deep down, I also resent the fact that I didn't know my father very well. I don't resent *him*, but there's always that envy of girls who actually have a father who gives them money and is always by their side. I feel like they had it too easy, like they're marshmallows.

GN: Would you have exchanged your father for anybody else?

JK: No! I realized from the very beginning that he was kind of a baby, and I didn't want to bring the harsh reality of my needs to him. I always thought he was elevated somewhere away from everything, that he sacrificed fatherhood for something grander. Besides, those were great times in the Lower East Side—drinking Lipton's tea and watching the cockroaches and eating Chef Boyardee spaghetti.

GN: How did you first meet your father?

JK: There was a paternity test to see if I was really his daughter. We met him out in Brooklyn with his lawyer. Jack was staggering around the street and acting like a real noodle brain. I was very proud of him—I figured he'd taken after me. His lawyer suggested we have lunch, and Jack instantly said, "Ah! There's a place!" and went right into a bar. The lawyer was making all kinds of objections, because he thought this little daughter would be shocked, but I'd been in millions of bars already. *Bar* was the first word I learned, by the way. In the bar, my mother was looking at him fondly, and he was making little marital jokes, like how she always used to burn the bacon. It was amazing to hear these episodes that went on while I was in the womb. It made me feel like I was a real human being, because I had little friends who had mothers *and* fathers—and I'd always just had a mother, with a father as a legendary figure out in the universe.

GN: How did he react to you?

JK: He acted like a shy boy on his first date. I had no shadow of a doubt that he was my father. It was just obvious to me, and I know it was obvious to him, too. But he had already told his mother that I wasn't his daughter, to protect her, and he didn't know how to get out of this lie. After the blood test, we went back to my neighborhood, and the first thing he wanted was to go to the liquor store. So I took him around the corner on Tenth Street, and he bought a bottle of Harveys Bristol Cream sherry, which I never forgot, because I kept the cork for years.

When he came up to our apartment, my little half sisters crowded around him. He opened the bottle of sherry and started playing with the little pieces of black plastic. He'd say, "Ugh! He's a Russian! See 'im? He's a Russian! He's no good!" and my little sisters would go into peals of laughter. It gave him a way of avoiding the more serious question of me. To my sisters he was just another funny guy, like the junkies and alcoholics who were always coming over, but to me he was my *very own* funny guy, because he was my father. When he left, I looked at the door in a daze as if I knew he was about to come back any minute, and he did. He said, "Whoops! I forgot my survival hat!" and we gave him his hat, and then he said, "Well, see ya in Janyary." Every once in a while I'd take out the cork and look at it, until I lost it like everything else.

GN: Did he ever admit he was your father?

JK: About a year later I phoned him, and we talked for hours. He was drunk, and so he was talking very freely, telling me about the family crest, referring to it as *your, our.* He also told me, "Remember, you're not a Canuck—you're a Bretonne."

GN: When did you first start reading his books?

JK: I never thought of them until I got hepatitis and went to Lincoln Hospital in the Bronx. My doctor noticed my name and said, "You ought to read *On the Road.*" He gave me a copy, and while I was there I read it. In later years I read a few more of his books, but I've never had an overwhelming curiosity about them. I'm coming out of the fountain rather than stumbling on it, dying of thirst. I feel like I already have all of his feelings and tendencies inside me.

GN: When did you see your father again?

JK: That was in '67, when I was about to go to Mexico. I'd been in the Bronx Youth House and I'd gotten pregnant and I was fifteen. I had to leave the country or else they were going to send me to Hudson Girls' Reformatory till I was twenty-one. Just for being pregnant I'd have to spend six years with a bunch of dykes!

First I went up to Lowell, because I *had* to see Jack one more time. I was with the man who was to become my first husband. We looked in the phone book and found all these Kerouacs, and I was really surprised, because in New York and everywhere else there were no names even similar. I thought, "Wow! This is like González in Mexico." We kept calling Kerouacs till we finally got one who spoke some English. It was Jack's cousin Harvey, and he and his wife spirited us over there, yelling, "Jack! Jack! Your daughter!" What I saw was Jack sitting in front of the television in this rocking chair, upending a quart bottle of whiskey. He was watching *The Beverly Hillbillies*. His mother, Gabrielle, was in the wheelchair because she had already had her stroke. He was married to Stella by that time, whom I instantly recognized as a mother figure for both of them, since he no longer had his mama to take care of him.

When I sat on the couch next to him, it reminded me of sitting down with an adolescent boy. He was afraid to look at me. The first thing I said to him was, "You know, my mother says we have very similar hands." So we looked at our hands, and he said, "Oh. Oh, yeah! Huh!" Meanwhile, one of the relatives found my boyfriend outside and brought him in. He had just come back from three years' traveling in Asia and had his hair in a bun. Jack said to him, "Ahhh? Genghis Khan?" We didn't know exactly what to say, but we just made conversation. He started telling us little amusing tales about these paintings on his wall. There was a painting of the Pope, which he'd done himself; then a drawing of Gerard, his brother; and then a painting of underwear hanging on a line. After a short while, his mother started raving about foreigners and about Caroline, Jack's sis-

223

ter, who had died. His mother was having strange visions that we were demons threatening her existence. Stella said, "You'll have to leave soon. Gabrielle may have another stroke." Before we left, Jack said, "Sure, you can go to Mexico. Use my name. Write a book." So we did write a novel when we were there, *The Influence*.

GN: How did you learn of his death?

JK: After my baby was stillborn, we came up to California. We were living in a commune in Little River. One day when I was working in the garden, a girl came running out of the house and said, "Jan! Your father just died! I heard it on the radio!" I see these tears in *her* eyes, because she's looking at me, expecting me to cry. But I just stood there and said, "Hmmm. Died, huh? Gee, that's strange." I must've seemed really cold to her, but I couldn't force myself to cry. The feeling I had was that I wanted to see him again, wanted to be his friend, or maybe his drinking buddy. I thought, "What did he have to go and do that for, the bum?"

GN: Since then, you seem to have found him chiefly by becoming him yourself. You've even written about your desire to be a man.

JK: If I'm not constantly remembering that I'm a woman, I tend to forget about it, and I just feel like a neuter being—especially when I'm traveling alone. As I wrote in "Everthreads," I'd be riding through South American cities and suddenly be jolted out of my reveries because some guys had noticed that I was female—and they'd be calling to me and making a big ruckus to announce their discovery. I wished I could blend in as a masculine bum, so I could just go through life and do things and nobody would bother me. But I also very often felt like I *was* my father. Maybe my soul is male.

GN: Did you ever find men who were threatened by your strength?

JK: Yeah, it's often under the surface. It's funny, I've been in more fights with men than with women. Of course, I was beaten up by women in the detention home in New York, and I can never muster up the courage to fight back when a woman is assaulting me. Maybe that has something to do with not having a father. But with men I'm very competitive and sometimes violent. I don't want to scare away all the men, but I remember one incident in Espanola, New Mexico, where I went to shoot pool in this bar. When my turn came up, I was playing with an old Mexican guy, and I won the game. He was very drunk and evidently had some complex about women. At the very end, he conveniently forgot which balls he had and thought he had the solids when he had the stripes, or vice versa, but everyone else was witnessing, and they knew which balls I had. He was disputing whether or not it was his turn to shoot the eight ball in, and I held my ground and said, "It's *my* turn." He got really mad and screamed, "No woman's gonna tell me . . . gonna push me around!" He was coming toward me menacingly, and just from instinct I pushed him away. Then he started brandishing his pool cue at me, and this fencing match ensued in which everyone jumped in and befriended me, and finally we just got thrown out.

GN: Speaking of balls, what do you think of Norman Mailer's saying that women can't write because they don't have any?

JK: It's just obviously not true, because women do write. Yet— well, maybe I shouldn't say this, but it's true that I haven't met as many women whose mentality I've respected as men. Men who haven't known many mentally stimulating women might easily make the generalization that women can't think. On the other hand, I was taken aback by an interview with Jorge Luis Borges, where he said that a student of his was one of the most intelligent women he'd run into but that she couldn't quite grasp some meaning in a book he was teaching. Then he started saying that women were incapable of thinking things out that far. He said women take the world for granted more than men—that women see themselves as actresses and have this shallow idea of how the world sees them. I was really enjoying the whole thing, and then I thought, "Well!" But then I thought, "Well, he's never met *me!*"

GN: You say you were never interested in women's liberation Why?

JK: Maybe it was because I was never looking for a career as a construction worker or a Safeway manager. I was always having jobs like dishwasher and cook. But it seems that if I have a strong feeling of independence in my own self, then that just sort of shows, and I don't have to go around screaming that I'm independent. There are more important things to scream about—animals being killed and the oceans being destroyed.

GN: Aren't dishwashers subjected to sexual harassment?

JK: They are, but it doesn't seem to matter. If you're a dishwasher, you're part of the lower class anyway, and you just have to go along with the whole kitchen scene. There's a way of turning around that sort of thing. I could just as well go up to men and harass them. In fact, I do that a lot. If guys are very bent on being nasty, I totally ignore them or go away. But cooks and dishwashers are constantly joking with each other, and there's a certain way of reacting. If you're the typical woman who goes, "Oooh! Stop it!" then they keep bugging you. But if you turn around and throw some mashed potatoes at them and you all wrestle and slide on the floor and spray each other with water and break dishes and prank around with them equally, then they realize that you're a different type of being.

GN: Artists *are* "a different type of being." But the problem, at least for your father, was that he couldn't have the best of both worlds—he couldn't remain free and creative and still be a father to you. Do you think it would be possible, or desirable, for you to get married and settle down?

JK: I've been married twice. The first marriage was longer and more successful; the second marriage was on a whim. But I still love both of my ex-husbands, and I'm good friends with both of them. I'm pretty partnership oriented, but I'm also very independent and headstrong. Even if I was married in the future, I would need at least a part of the house that was completely mine, a place where I could retreat and be a hermit sometimes. I like to sleep alone, as a matter of fact. Not always, but most of the time I do, because I have a certain rapport with my dreams. It's hard for me to remember my dreams when I wake up if I'm with somebody else in bed—because I tend to start talking to them right away or whatever, and my dreams just go all to hell, which is disquieting.

GN: It would be even harder to stay in touch with your dream life if you had children.

JK: I wouldn't want to have children until I had some land and a stable sort of condition for a child to grow up in. If I had a child right now, it would be inconvenient for both of us, because I still want to travel a lot. But I've known women who travel with their children, and those children are destined to grow up in that situation. A lot of people would say it is not good for a child to grow up in the slums of New York. I grew up in the slums of New York, and yet I'm not ruined. I know there are a lot of artists who are bringing up children and create at the same time. My father was just unable to face having a child. He had a lot of problems, a lot of guilt about his mother. Maybe if things had been a little different and he had had some prompting, he might've gotten in touch with me—but it just never happened.

My own life would have been very different if my daughter that I had when I was fifteen had lived. She would be almost twelve years old, probably be as tall as I am. But then where is the *if* in the universe? Does it exist anywhere? Can you say, "*If* this had happened, this would be like this"? I don't know.

Interview with Dianne Jones, May 2, 1996

Dianne Jones, an actress in the employ of an Italian film company, conducted this interview by telephone from her hotel room in San Francisco; Jan was at home in Albuquerque. This was the last interview Jan gave before falling ill and being hospitalized at Lovelace Hospital on May 10, 1996. She died after removal of her spleen on June 5.

DJ: So, we stuck you at home all night tonight?

JK: Well, I was going to stay home anyway.

DJ: Did you watch *Seinfeld*?

JK: Yeah.

DJ: Listen, I talked to Gerry about a lot of things today.[1] And he told me that you wanted to talk pretty much about the same things—about the Sampas family, about what's going on with your case. He pretty much brought us up to date about the actions that you've taken and the papers that you've filed and things of that nature. Can you kind of go back to the beginning and tell me how this all started.

JK: Well, I've known Gerry for a long time, for like twenty years. I met him originally when he came up to Washington State to interview my mother for his book, *Memory Babe*.[2] I can't even remember all the details of all the things that we've done together. It's just been a long friendship.

But recently—I think it was in '95—he had suggested a certain lawyer for me, for various reasons.[3] We met the lawyer at his house and also the lawyer's wife, who was really nice. Tom Brill and his wife,

Notes by Gerald Nicosia

[1]The Italian film crew was not able to get down to New Mexico to film Jan, so she sent them to film me in California, asking me to explain her cause and her legal case in her place. They had left my home earlier that day.

[2]Actually we met at Carol Ross's apartment in San Francisco the week before.

[3]I suggested Tom Brill to her in December 1993, and they met at my house in January 1994.

Marta, who is also his paralegal. I was sitting with Marta, just conversing and chatting. There was this huge pile of papers on the table in front of us. We had all these legal papers already out that we were just looking at. All of a sudden Marta noticed Gabrielle's will—my father's mother's will—and I looked at it, too. We both looked at it and said, "Gee, that's a really strange-looking signature. That doesn't even look real." We both remarked that it looked forged. Then we called Gerry and Tom to look at it. It was just a Xerox of the will. Then we realized, *Hey!* This is definitely a forgery. I mean, we felt that it was.

And so we looked into a handwriting analyst. He swears up and down it's a forgery. So we've got our experts. That was the beginning of my decision to sue the Sampas family for forging my grandmother's will. That's what I'm alleging that they did.

DJ: Have you taken anything to court?

JK: The whole thing is just totally happening, as much as it possibly can be. The trouble is, the Sampases continue to file motions to dismiss, of course. Because, I believe, they know what they did and they have no excuse. But they've got millions of dollars as a result, and they don't want to let go of it.

DJ: Who is helping you besides Gerry?

JK: Well, I've got five lawyers. Herbert Jacoby in New York, who's my copyright lawyer. I've got Thomas Brill, my main lawyer, but they filed some kind of stupid thing that makes him not able to be my lawyer—I don't exactly understand how it works, but because of a conflict of interest that they dug up. They want to dig up every teeny, nitpicky thing they can think of, of course, to delay us and screw us up. So he can't speak for me now. There's another lawyer, Ray Boucher, and Nat Hines. That's basically my lawyers, right there.

DJ: How have your father's friends reacted to all this, Jan?

JK: My father's friends? Well, unfortunately, there's a very tiny amount of true friends left. They've all gone over with the Sampases, because they're the guys with the money and the influence. Ferlinghetti is no longer my friend. Allen Ginsberg is no longer my friend, which is really tragic because I've known Allen Ginsberg for thirty-five years—more than that. I've been saying that for five years, so it must be forty years now.

DJ: How has Allen reacted to this? Have you spoken to him?

JK: Well, yeah. He was the first to know. I called him in Berlin. I found out that he was in Berlin at the time, in January of 1995.[4] He was my godfather, and I had lived with him, and I had done Buddhism, tried to sit in the lotus position and all that. He was actually teaching me. I said, "Allen, you know, I've discovered that my grandmother's will was a forgery, and I'm going to sue the Sampases." Immediately, his reaction was, "Oh, don't do that. That would be ugly, ugly, ugly." Those were his words, exactly. And then every time I saw him, every time until now, he's totally been sitting on the fence, not acknowledging what's happening, and totally, obviously, with the Sampases, doing all these things—his Whitney Museum exhibit and talking at NYU. And he led the audience to kick me out of NYU one time with Gerry.

DJ: Yes, I heard about that.

JK: And also, one time, we asked him, "What do you think of this systematic selling off of your best friend Jack's archive?" He said, "Oh, I'm a Buddhist. I don't care if the world blows up tomorrow." That was his reaction.

DJ: I see.

JK: He just turns his face, and he just won't say anything. He just says these cryptic little sayings to avoid the truth. Which I think is really reprehensible, considering that Jack really championed the truth. He's probably rolling in his grave to think that all these people who are supposedly his friends are now selling out, completely.

DJ: How do you think this battle is going to end, Jan?

JK: I certainly hope and pray that I win. What I want to do is, I don't want to just get all the stuff that the Sampases have and keep it

[4]Actually 1994.

for myself and sell it off like they're doing. What I want to do is put it in a museum. I'm very clear about which museum I want it to be, which is the Bancroft Library in Berkeley. And I know the curator, Tony Bliss. We've pledged it to him, because I want it to be in an archive for the public and everyone who loves Kerouac to be able to go and see. Whereas now, it's just in the hands of John Sampas and the rest of his family in Lowell, Massachusetts. They're controlling everything—very controlling.

I got this idea when I was down in Key West, Florida, in '93. I was walking along, and I saw the Hemingway House. I thought, *Wow!* I actually went on a tour and saw all of it. Everything's in its place. There are dynasties of cats that Hemingway had. I thought, *How nice. Why isn't there a Kerouac house?* I hadn't started the suit by then, but I was just thinking about it and thinking there really should be a house. Maybe in Lowell, or maybe in Nashua, even better. Because that's a place that Kerouac had a lot of ties to and a very emotional connection with. It's where his mother and father and brother are buried.

That was a recent thing also, that I tried to get his body moved from Lowell. Did you know about that?

DJ: What's that about?

JK: I don't think that Jack's body should be in Lowell, being desecrated every day by people who come to see the grave and leave wine bottles and candles and cigarette butts. I think it should be in St. Louis de Gonzague Cemetery in New Hampshire,[5] which he wrote about a lot. He even wrote about the actual cemetery. Anyway, it's all very complicated. There's a lot of press all about that, making me out to be some kind of a grave robber. You know, saying: "Kerouac's daughter wants to move writer's body to Nashua."

What happened was this Lowell City Council, that Sampas totally rules somehow with his influence, just had a meeting without me

---

[5]Jan's ashes were interred in St. Louis de Gonzague on June 5, 1997, but her father's body remains in the Sampas family plot in Edson Cemetery in Lowell.

even there or involved or anything and just decided, "We've decided that Jan Kerouac doesn't have the right to move the body." But daughters and sons move their parents' bodies all the time up there, everywhere.

DJ: Of course. I don't see why that's such a problem.

JK: See, they feel that they *own* him. Body and soul and everything. And all of the things that he had, all of his archive and shoes and raincoat and everything else under the sun. I don't like their attitude. It's funny, because a lot of people tell me, "Oh, come on. Why don't you just be nice and have a settlement?" Well, sure. I would, except . . . they've completely trod on me. Here I am on life support, and they've taken away half my income.[6] I mean, I'm not about to cozy up to them after all this. They've been totally evil to me.

DJ: Jan, what do you personally have left of your dad?

JK: Nothing. Absolutely nothing. Just his DNA. I mean, I'm the spitting image of him.

DJ: I know. I saw the photographs today, by the way. They're lovely.

JK: Oh, good. The very first time I met him, it was for a blood test. That was my mother's doing. She was trying to determine for the courts that I was his daughter, so that he would have to pay child support. I didn't have any hand in that. I was just excited because it was the first time I met my father.

DJ: How did that meeting go?

JK: Oh, it was great. It stands out in my memory like a shining beacon. Actually, I wrote about it in my book *Baby Driver*. It made me feel like I was a real human being, to know that I had a mother and a father after all. I had always felt kind of like a freak not knowing my father, like maybe I didn't deserve to live or something. But I had all

---

[6]John Sampas had recently instructed agent Sterling Lord to stop paying Jan a sizable portion of the royalty income from her father that she had been receiving for the past ten years.

kinds of funny ideas about that. I took him to a liquor store, and he got a bottle of Harveys Bristol Cream sherry. Anyway.

DJ: You met him another time after that, right?

JK: A second time, and last time. Up in Lowell, before I went to Mexico. He was there with Stella, his nursemaid, who . . . I'd better not say anything because of the case. I know—and a lot of people have told me, too, who were very close to him—that he married Stella [because] she was a girl that he had known growing up in Lowell, all his life, kind of a plain Jane who knew and wanted to marry him. He finally married her because he needed her to take care of his mother, Gabrielle, who had had a stroke and was in a wheelchair. And who, previous to the stroke, had always taken care of Jack. He was a complete mama's boy. In fact, that's part of the reason why he never acknowledged me as his daughter, because he never told his mother that I was his daughter. He was afraid to admit it, and he was very guilt ridden about that whole thing.

DJ: How do you feel about him, Jan?

JK: Oh, I love him. And I'm trying to restore his dignity and the family name. In fact, a whole bunch of French Canadians are coming down from Canada this October, when Gerry and I are going to Lowell again to speak.[7] I'm quite certain that they're going to be behind me, because there are hundreds of Kerouacs in Quebec and they don't want their name besmirched. They don't want one of their own geniuses, who started out with the French language and became a classic American writer, to be shat upon. And that's what's happening, even twenty-seven years after his death. Even hypocrites like Allen Ginsberg, who claims to be the figurehead of the Beat genera-

---

[7]Lowell Corporation for the Humanities president Brad Parker had already rented the hall at Middlesex College for us to speak during Kerouac Week, since the official Kerouac Committee, closely affiliated with the Sampas family, had ignored us for the past eight years. The "whole bunch of French Canadians" she refers to are members of L'Association des Familles Kirouac, led by founding president Jacques Kirouac from Quebec City, one of Jan's closest friends at the end of her life.

tion, or something. It's atrocious what's happening. I haven't been able to do anything, because even with five lawyers, they've got the dough. They've got endless, endless money to pay . . . lawyers to keep the truth from coming out.

DJ: The truth as you tell it will certainly come out in this documentary.[8]

JK: Oh, good.

DJ: I don't know how much good that will do you, but it can't hurt.

JK: No, it's great.

DJ: Is there anything that you'd like to add? Is there anything we can do for you? Is there anything special that you'd like to say?

JK: Well, I know that this new generation of Xers, or whatever you want to call them, that are coming up now have a very uncanny affection for the Beats and for Jack Kerouac in particular. I would like to help in leaving the legacy to them and to all people who appreciate the Beat generation and what it signifies, and the wild, spontaneous prose that my father started, so that these evil people don't wind up just completely ruining the whole thing by stealing. It's like a stolen legacy. I might just die in the process. That's very possible because of my condition. But even if I do, I want to make sure that it's carried on and that my father's name is finally honored and the whole thing goes down in history as being . . . that I resurrected, or helped to resurrect, his dignity and his honor.

DJ: Well, Jan, I think you're on a very noble, noble cause. I wish you the best of luck with this battle and your own personal battles. I know that you aren't well, and I know that you don't have that much support around you. You have a few people who are willing to help you or that can help you.

---

[8]In fact, the documentary they produced for the 1996 Venice Biennale film festival said nothing about Jan. The material about her was all cut.

JK: Mostly Gerry is the one who winds up helping me the most, from afar.

DJ: We'll be in touch. I'll make sure that you get a copy of this documentary in your hands. If I may, I'd like to write you from Rome.

JK: Oh, great.

DJ: If there's anything that I can do, I want you to call me. I'll give you my number.

JK: The other thing I just wanted to say is I would actually like to challenge Allen Ginsberg to announce publicly why it is that he is not helping Jack Kerouac's daughter at all, even though I've known him for forty years and I was so close to him before. Why this sudden turning his back on me? I just don't understand it. I'd like him to say why it is.

DJ: Jan, he is going to get a copy of this documentary, too, so he'll hear your challenge.[9]

JK: Okay. And you'll send me a copy of Gerry's video?[10]

DJ: Absolutely.

JK: Great. I'll really look forward to seeing it.

DJ: All right. You take care of yourself, and I wish you the best of luck.

JK: Thanks. You too.

DJ: Thank you, Jan. Thanks a lot.

[9]As far as I know, Ginsberg never received this interview. He died less than a year after Jan's death, on April 5, 1997.
[10]The interview they had just filmed with me.

Memoir of Jan Kerouac
by Marjorie Van Halteren

I was raised in a family where the concept of a steady job and a home were tantamount to religion. At the present time, I have neither. In fact, my husband and I don't have much, save a collection of boxes, awaiting shipment overseas, somewhere on a pier in Brooklyn. For the two of us have finally taken the plunge we've talked about for so many years: we've moved to France, in search of creative career opportunities and the promise of decent living for both of us.

The transition was relatively smooth at first, but then a job fell through, in very untimely fashion, at the start of August. There we were, left anxiously cooling our heels in the Provençal sun, while all of France frolicked on vacation.

Suddenly, with little to do, I just can't stop thinking about Jan, whom I met around 1982. I had been rummaging through the Ks in the fiction section of a large bookstore, preparing a radio program on Jack Kerouac, when I fell upon *Baby Driver: A Novel About Myself* by Jan Michele Kerouac. She turned out to be Jack's legitimate daughter, and eventually I made the program about her. Maybe it was because, interested as I was in the Beats, I was tired of their male domination. Maybe it was because I liked her first book, and her second, for the frankness, the spirit of it. Maybe it was because Jan, although not raised by, and therefore hardly in a position to be influenced by, Jack, turned out to be his true heir after all, reveling in extraordinary wordplay and the random poetry of life. Even her letters are littered with it, underscored by the miraculous snapshots, often of blue water and endless skies, that she takes wherever she goes, tucked inside the envelope as afterthoughts. I soon forgot all about Jack, and soon she became just my friend Jan.

After phone calls and correspondence, we finally met over a dinner in Santa Fe, that time we were passing through. Yes, Jan and I both liked words, traveling, and Mexican food. Yes, we were born the same year. Yes, with our long dark hair and bangs, that picture of her on *Baby Driver* could be me. But we were quite reserved with each other, sensing the natural differences, too—until the day she showed up on our doorstep, very unexpectedly. After that we had an ongoing connection. She'd come to stay from time to time, jokingly calling me and my husband "Mom and Dad," until I (not so jokingly) asked her not to.

I cannot escape admitting it: my feelings about her have always been ragingly ambivalent. It's that middle-class religion. I was raised in suburban Detroit, in upper-middle-class security, with two parents, my own room, a big yard. She was raised on the Lower East Side of Manhattan, in tenements, with no father. She got her own room once because the wall to the abandoned apartment next door had fallen down. She never seemed to have money, a real job, real plans, and what's more, she never seemed particularly worried about it. I, on the other hand, was fixated on getting along and getting ahead. She was solely interested in getting through the next couple of weeks or so, and having a good time.

It wasn't that she was unreliable, exactly, or dishonest. In fact, she usually gave us things, cooking and baking up a storm. On your worst day, Jan would spend her last dollar on red roses, or on special flour for her croissants, because the kind in your pantry wasn't just right. And there were what my husband called "Jan's little gifts," things she simply left behind. Mostly they were the extra weight she was forced to shed in her continual trek around the world: a piece of pottery, a souvenir pen, a pair of shoes she could no longer squeeze into the side pockets of that ubiquitous black duffel bag. Once, in the absence of Jan, a Jan letter arrived, with the following P.S. scrawled on the back: "Oh! Did anyone see a big, black shirt? Maybe I left it on the floor of the world." I mused to myself: yes, she dances all night at the world, she goes to sleep in Albuquerque . . . wakes up in the Mexican jungle . . . stumbles into a New Orleans kitchen, to fix herself a cup of jet-black coffee . . . but her laundry lives in Brooklyn, with us. . . . My husband reminded me that the World was the name of a discotheque in New York.

What about the time she worked her magic on an old friend of mine, luring him to Peru of all places, and abandoned him there, high up in the Andes, because (she said) he just wouldn't stop "complaining"? What about the time I took her to my favorite little neighborhood place for lunch, thinking she'd really enjoy it, and instead she engaged the waitress in a lengthy philosophical discussion on the exact reasons why, no matter what, the stuff we had just been served was *not* cappuccino, and never would be, in its wildest dreams, because if she knew *one* thing . . .

She knew a thing or two, and she's been on my mind constantly, ever since the other day, when I was sitting on a sizzling curb in Aix-en-Provence, waiting for my husband to make his umpteenth phone call from a public telephone, in an attempt to jump-start our lives. I was even wearing a kind of Jan outfit—stretch tank top and white pants—and doing a supremely Jan thing—counting out the number of francs I had in my change purse, proudly thinking, whadda pile, out loud, the way she used to do, while I, across the room, would grit my teeth and wonder if she wanted to borrow money. She never asked directly, but she'd take it if offered and pay it back. Eventually.

Hearing myself, I suddenly thought back to another phone booth. This time, Jan's in the booth, the booth's in Honolulu. It was the time she tried for real to move permanently to Hawaii. Jan always said she just wasn't comfortable too far away from the sea. "I just gotta be able to jump in the ocean once in a while," she would say.

This was also the one time she did ask me flat out for money. And the time I decided I was going to do her a favor, damn it, be really firm this time, be once and for all the responsible grown-up. I said no.

It was a long time before I heard from her again. But at last I did, and I was glad. Although, the last time I saw her, she particularly drove me crazy. In New York for a visit from Puerto Rico, she spent all her money in two days, and when I got back from a long, frustrating day at work I discovered that she had been forced to waste her entire third day in our apartment, waiting for the UPS man to bring cash in crisp twenty-dollar bills—sent by a savior by the sea.

The two of us went out for a late dinner, and by the time we turned down Henry Street for the long walk home, it was midnight. We didn't have much to say, our feet beating out an exhausted mantra on the cracked Brooklyn sidewalk. The moon was shining, full and surreal. Then we smelled fresh bread baking, and I just caved in. I thought, oh hell, there is no good reason to be doing anything else in the whole world, is there, but walking with Jan, at midnight in Brooklyn, smelling fresh bread, and I told her so. She replied that no one else ever just walked with her, smelling bread and talking about it like that, not even her many boyfriends, and she liked me for that. And because I talked to her about writing. Her writing.

She left again the next day. That afternoon, desperate for cappuccino, I sneaked out of my hectic job. I found the perfect little café table, forgetting about my telephone. The little spoon the waiter brought, it was so solid, and the foam piled in a high dome, excellent. I really hate it when it's flat. This is when it truly struck me exactly what Jan and I have in common. She knows that each day is a vessel, holding nothing but itself, no matter where you're going, or where you've been. And each day flows by, never to return. Now, it was Jack's voice, so uncannily like Jan's, that I could hear, from a record I had, saying, "Sometimes I'm walking on the ground, and I look down and I see right through the ground, and there *is* no world, but you'll find out, you'll find out." He dumped Jan into that world, where she does the backstroke.

Where is Jan now? I guess I lost her again. I can imagine her living by the sea—but that hardly narrows it down. Holding on to her is like trying to ride a dolphin; she's slippery. Perhaps she'll show up one more time. Her arrivals are a bit like the way she takes life, moment to moment, just connect the dots, islands in the stream. Here, landlocked, so far from familiar shores, I can almost hear the ocean roar.

August 1992

Jack Kerouac's Estate[1]

When he died in 1969, the Beat author Jack Kerouac left behind a house in St. Petersburg, Fla., countless letters and papers, a following of passionate readers and a daughter he had met just twice. Now his daughter, Jan, is accusing the Kerouac estate, which is administered by John Sampas, Kerouac's former brother-in-law, of breaking up the estate by selling off pieces for profit.

Ms. Kerouac has sued in state court in Florida, stating that when Kerouac's mother died in 1973, her will, which left her son's possessions to the Sampas family, was illegally drawn up. The estate should belong to her, she says. "The purpose of gaining control isn't just money, but so that I can get all of my father's possessions into one archive and sell them to a museum or library," she said in an interview yesterday.

It's hard to keep track of what has become of all of Kerouac's belongings, but it's clear from his letters that the author wanted them kept together. George Tobla Jr., a lawyer for the Boston firm of Burns & Levinson, which is representing the Kerouac estate, says his clients are trying to keep the most important items intact. The items that are meaningful from a literary or scholarly standpoint—including letters from Kerouac to a fellow Beat, the poet Allen Ginsberg, and manuscripts of Kerouac's books, including "On the Road"—are in such public institutions as the New York Public Library, he said.[2]

If other things come on the market, Mr. Tobia added, that doesn't mean much. For example, in a recent sale that Ms. Kerouac said made her furious, the actor Johnny Depp bought a raincoat of Kerouac's.[3]

---

[1]From "Book Notes" by Sarah Lyall, *New York Times*, May 25, 1994.
[2]The manuscript of *On The Road* was kept in a display case at the New York Public Library for about a year. Currently this manuscript, like the majority of other manuscripts of Kerouac's books, is not available for study.
[3]Jan was not especially bothered by the sale of the raincoat or other clothing items. What deeply troubled her was learning from dealer Jeffrey Weinberg that manuscripts, notebooks, letters, and her father's books were also being sold off.

"You couldn't have treasured items more cared for than the estate is caring for them," Mr. Tobia said. "They're not going to treat every shred of clothing he ever donned or touched as if it was the Shroud of Turin."

The dispute is in some respects a typical case of the arguments that can take place after an author dies and leaves potentially lucrative effects behind. It's all the more difficult because of the tenuous connections with Kerouac: Jan's mother, Joan Haverty, was separated from Kerouac soon after their marriage; Stella Sampas, John Sampas's sister, married Kerouac several years before he died. (She died in 1990.)

Meanwhile, the estate is accusing Ms. Kerouac of greed, Ms. Kerouac is accusing the estate of greed and Kerouac scholars are weighing in with their own views. Gerald Nicosia, who wrote a biography of Kerouac in 1983 and who supports Ms. Kerouac, said in an interview that Ms. Kerouac had been severely mistreated by the estate. And, he said, the public had a right to see the entire Kerouac archive. "I believe that once all these manuscripts are available, we'll get rid of this myth that he was just a barbarian who produced this stuff off the top of his head," he said.

On the Road to Daddy[1]

Jan Kerouac first met her father Jack when she was nine years old. He arrived at her mother's apartment in New York's shabby East Village, and immediately asked: "Where's the liquor store?" Jan took his hand and led him to the shop. He bought some Harvey's Bristol Cream sherry and drank the entire bottle that afternoon in their living room.

This was not an auspicious first meeting for father and daughter. Kerouac had suddenly become famous as the icon of the Beat generation after the publication of *On The Road*, and he was in downtown New York that afternoon in 1961 to take the blood test which would prove that Jan was his daughter, and indeed his only child. He had divorced his wife, Joan Haverty Kerouac, when she was pregnant with Jan.[2] The paternity test ensured that he paid $12 a week in child support.

Twenty-five years after Kerouac's death, Jan is still trying to hold on to her father, both emotionally and financially. She has just begun legal action disputing his mother Gabrielle's will, which gave everything to Kerouac's third wife, Stella Sampas. (Kerouac died of alcohol-related disease long before his mother.) Jan has shown the will to legal handwriting experts who claim Gabrielle's signature is a forgery, and that Kerouac appears to be spelt incorrectly. One witness to the will also says he never saw it signed. Jan says: "It's not a money issue. I make a comfortable living from my father's book royalties and my own work. I just don't want to see my father's precious letters and paintings and goods sold off piecemeal to private buyers. I want it all to be kept together in a proper Kerouac museum in one of his old houses—like the Hemingway museum in his house in Florida."

The Sampas family have sold off individual items belonging to Kerouac—there is a lucrative market in beatnik nostalgia. His tweed coat went for $50,000 to the actor Johnny Depp, and signed docu-

---

[1]Kate Muir, *London Times*, June 10, 1994
[2]Jack Kerouac left Joan a month after she got pregnant, but they did not divorce until 1957.

ments, letters and books from his library have also been sold. They have a vault full of Kerouac's rarely-displayed primitive, swirling paintings. The Sampases also own Kerouac's 19 book drafts, including the famous manuscript of *On The Road*, written non-stop on a roll of teletype paper so that he wasted no time changing the sheets in his typewriter.

Jan Kerouac is bringing the suit against the Sampas family along with Kerouac's nephew's son, Paul Blake III, the other surviving blood relative. A letter from Kerouac, written the day before his death and quoted by his biographers, also indicates he did not want the Sampas family to inherit.

He wrote this to his nephew, Paul Blake Jr: "Dear Little Paul: This is Uncle Jack. I've turned over my entire estate, real, personal and mixed, to Memere [mother], and if she dies before me, it is then turned to you, and if I die thereafter, it all goes to you . . . I just wanted to leave my estate to someone directly connected with the last remaining drop of my direct blood line, which is, me sister Carolyn, your Mom, and not to leave a dingblasted f***ing goddamn thing to my wife's one hundred Greek relatives. I also plan to divorce, or have her marriage to me annulled. Just telling you the facts of how it is . . ."[3]

Note that there is no mention of Jan Kerouac here—the book royalties come to her automatically, but Kerouac appears to have wanted his nephew to have the rest. The "one hundred Greek relatives" may have a genuine claim, since Stella Sampas nursed Gabrielle Kerouac for three years before her death, and Mrs Kerouac may have decided to change the will. The Sampas family will not discuss the matter, but their lawyer has dismissed the claim as "baseless and frivolous" and said there was nothing wrong with selling off Kerouac's shoes (at $3,000 a pair) or clothing: "Not every shred has to be treated like the Shroud of Turin."

[3]This letter, Jack Kerouac to Paul Blake, Jr., October 20, 1969, is currently on deposit in the Berg Collection of the New York Public Library.

Jan, now 42, left home as a teenager and roamed around the country rather like her father. She also became an alcoholic for a time, and first read *On The Road* in psychiatric care, aged 14. "It explained a lot to me about the weird way I thought." She moved to Albuquerque in New Mexico, became teetotal and wrote two semi-autobiographical novels, *Baby Driver* and *Trainsong*. She undergoes dialysis for failed kidneys every day, but she has also just finished a third book, *Parrot Fever*.[4]

Jan is being supported in her fight over the will by Gerald Nicosia, one of Kerouac's biographers, but other friends, such as the poet Allen Ginsberg, are, she says, "turning a blind eye to the whole thing," not wanting to upset relations with the Sampas family who control access to many documents. She chose to announce the legal suit at a Beat generation conference last month, celebrating the fiftieth anniversary of the meeting of Ginsberg, Kerouac and William Burroughs. Although Ginsberg talked about the "intergenerational transmission of sympathy" this did not seem to include Jan Kerouac.

Despite failing health, putting together a shrine of some sort to Kerouac has become an obsession for his daughter, an attempt to gain the control after death that she never had during his life. The second and last time Jan saw her father was aged 15 at his mother's house. "By that time he was constantly drinking. He was on the couch with a bottle of whiskey. I went up to him and said: 'My mother says we have the same hands,' and I held out my palms. He was very bashful about it, like a little boy on a first date. I think he felt guilty because he had never acknowledged my existence to his mother in the beginning." Jan told him she was going to Mexico to have a baby (which was stillborn) and to write.

Kerouac said: "Yeah, you go to Mexico, write a book. You can use my name."

---

[4] Jan did not finish *Parrot Fever*.

Jan Kerouac, the only child of Beat generation novelist Jack Kerouac, was born on February 16, 1952, in Albany, New York. Her mother was Jack Kerouac's second wife, Joan Haverty. Jan's mother and father separated before she was born, and Jan was raised mostly on New York City's Lower East Side. She did not meet her father until 1962, when they were both compelled to take blood tests as part of a paternity suit brought by Joan to obtain child support. Jan met her father only once more, while on her way to Mexico at the age of fifteen. At that point, she had already been in and out of various detention facilities and sought to avoid several more years of incarceration at the Bronx Youth House.

On her return to the States in 1968, when she was just sixteen years old, Jan married writer and occultist John Lash in San Francisco. They migrated to a hippie commune in Little River, California—where she learned of her father's death on the radio—then to her mother's new home in Kittitas, Washington. After she and John separated, Jan moved to Santa Fe, New Mexico, and from there began an extensive journey through Mexico and Central and South America. During those travels, she began to write seriously.

Returning to live with her mother in Washington in the mid-1970s, Jan got married for a second time, to Bernard Hackett, and the two traveled to North Africa and England. That marriage also lasted only a couple of years, and Jan resumed wandering the country, always carrying her manuscripts with her. *Baby Driver*, originally called "Everthreads," was completed in Ellensburg, Washington, at the start of 1980 and published the following year by St. Martin's Press. Her second novel, *Trainsong*, the record of several more years of restless travels and dozens more men, was published by Henry Holt in 1988.

During the 1980s, Jan gained some reputation as a poet and even more notoriety as a participant in many Beat and Kerouac conferences, including the *On the Road* twenty-fifth anniversary celebration at the Naropa Institute in Boulder, Colorado, the One World Poetry Festival in Amsterdam, the Rencontre Internationale Jack Kerouac in

Quebec City, and the events surrounding the dedication of the commemorative to her father in Lowell, Massachusetts. She also contributed liner notes to the *Jack Kerouac Collection*, rare recordings by her father issued by Rhino Records in 1990.

In 1991, at the age of thirty-nine, Jan suffered complete kidney failure in Puerto Rico, necessitating her to do peritoneal dialysis four times a day for the rest of her life. Despite the physical hardship imposed by her illness, she continued to work on a third novel, "Parrot Fever," which was unfinished at the time of her death. She also undertook a monumental legal battle to recover, preserve, and make accessible the entire literary archive of her father—an effort she also did not live to complete. She died of complications following surgery in Lovelace Hospital in Albuquerque on June 5, 1996, at the age of forty-four.